"*Insightful and enlightening book of* empowering exercises. *I loved it, Bravo.*"

ROSANNA LO MEO-PEACHEY,
a Life Transformed Life Coach, Breathwork, Healing and author
of *A Little Bit of Heaven*

"*You will see your deep questions asked— and then explored, through Tricia's vulnerable and genuine sharing of her own questing and expansive discoveries.*"

LESLIE S. BLACK
Heart Awakening Transformational Coaching & Energy Healing,
LIFE TRANSFORMED Certified Coach

"*Do yourself a divine favor, and read this brilliant book. You will laugh, cry, and learn how to move from being Eeyore to Cosmic Tigger as easily as an exhale. In these nurturing and enlightening pages, Tricia's warm, wise voice invites you to fall into a huge, loving space, and awaken all the way through to the infinite joy that you are. "Nudge me lightly. I'm listening now." Yes, Tricia, so am I, and so will you be after reading this book!*"

CHRISTINE W. ELDER,
Awakening Guide, Sound Healer, Transformational Coach

"*Tricia Croyle has written a must-read book for anyone desiring to be a beacon of joy and transformation on this planet. She illuminates that your journey matters. Allow Tricia's words to guide you in discovering the beauty of your unique path.*"

NIKOLE KADEL,
Ecologist, Natural Healer, Global Consciousness Leader

FROM
Heartache
TO
Joy

One Woman's Journey Home

TRICIA JEANE CROYLE

The teachings of Rikka Zimmerman are paraphrased here with the kind permission of Rikka Zimmerman

Copyright © 2018 by Tricia Jeane Croyle

Book cover and interior design by Christina Gaugler

Library of Congress Cataloging-in-Publication Data: 2017918857

ISBN 978-1-7330509-2-0

Silver Creek Books
N7938 Hwy D, Algoma, WI 54201

ACKNOWLEDGMENTS

I would like to thank my mother, for the lifelong lessons she shared, especially the gratitude that she showed each day toward the end of her life. My husband, for his perseverance in fighting the good fight for clean water and a healthy environment, and also for allowing me to be me. Rikka Zimmerman, for opening the door to me discovering my true nature. My fellow LT coaches, for encouraging me to put myself out there.

CONTENTS

FOREWORD

Settle into a comfy chair in a beautiful space, favorite beverage nearby, and take a few slow deep breaths.... Then open yourself to a time of sublime conversation with the delightful Tricia Jeane Croyle.

I have had the blessing of many such conscious conversations in person with Tricia, and I can assure you this book expresses her true voice, unedited! Through her most unique vibration, Tricia brings refreshing expansive insights and reflections that are somehow both earthy and ethereal, both practical and magical, both whimsical and wise.

You will see your deep questions asked— and then explored, through Tricia's vulnerable and genuine sharing of her own questing and expansive discoveries.

You will experience some of her magical visions and dreams, that grace a dull day with sunshine and color.

You will collect a treasure trove of true gems of deep wisdom, often packaged in catchy quotes to post on your mirror as reminders.

I recommend using this book like spiritual mentoring sessions that include meditation space. Perhaps gift yourself with a chapter a day (or even better, a chapter a week), breathe in and savor the buffet of rich offerings, and give yourself space to digest the profound, tasty morsels into your being and your life. And leave lots of space for both laughter and awe.

You have here 18 expansive mentoring sessions with this honest, funny, and deeply wise woman, opening into your own joy and magic! Enjoy each step of your journey... and laugh heartily!

Leslie Sandra Black
Victoria, BC, Canada

INTRODUCTION:
The Fortune Cookie

It began with a fortune cookie.

It was Saturday date night: Chinese buffet and a movie. I grabbed a fortune cookie on the way out, and stopped to read it. Then I handed it to John, my husband—the cookie was obviously meant for him. Sometimes I get his cookie instead of mine.

Then I saw another fortune cookie on the ground. It was still in its plastic bag and in crumbs from being stepped on. I picked it up, opened it, and read the fortune. It was the same fortune that I had selected in the restaurant, and given to my husband.

Or did it select me?

It said, "You have a charming way with words. You should write a book."

The fortune cookie gnawed away at me long after I had gnawed away at it. I told myself, *Not me! I can't. I don't know how! John is the writer.*

My mother was also a writer. I had spent my whole life denying that I could write. Professionally, I could write just fine—well enough for an architect. But the fortune had said that I should write a book. What about?

The universe is not to be denied, in my experience. We deny the universe and God at our own peril. So here goes. The universe has spoken and is speaking through me. It is the way of the muse. How a*mus*ing.

BACKGROUND

This book is a combination of ideas and stories—many from webinars, classes, and books by Rikka Zimmerman, Kenji Kumara, Ester Hicks, and Zach Rehder. I have dated and attributed the ideas wherever possible. The "what if" questions are often stimulated by the ideas of Rikka. When I use the word "quantum," it comes from Kenji. When I talk about the vortex or being in alignment, it's likely from Ester Hicks.

I believe that thoughts hang out in the "noosphere," a word that I came across many years ago. Thoughts hang out there and become available to all of us almost simultaneously. That is why many great writers and spiritualists write books on the same topic at the same time. Knowing this, who originated the idea becomes muddled. I want to give credit to people for their ideas and not take credit for them as my own. But I also don't want to put words into their mouths that they might not have said, or to misrepresent their ideas.

Sometimes I hear something. I write it down and then I interpret it. It becomes changed as it moves through my experience of it. Like the game of Telephone: when the message gets to the end, it's nothing like when it started out.

Often I wear others' ideas like a cloak: I put it on, wear it around for a while, and see how it feels. If I like it, I put it in my closet, so that I can put it on whenever I want. When it becomes old and worn, I throw it away.

When ideas came from a class, webinar, or a YouTube video, I've noted this and dated them (within a day or two of when I experienced them). However, they are in no way a transcription of that event or video. Often, they are ideas I jotted down that resonated with me. I said to myself, *How interesting. I'll write that down. I want to remember that.* When the idea is extensive, I have paraphrased and indented it.

Or, sometimes what was said meant something else to me. I was reminded of my own idea about that topic. My dreams, visions, and journeys are also noted, and the actual vision is differentiated from my interpretation of it—so that the reader may know that this is what I saw, and this is what I think about what I saw. I am intending to show the growth in my understanding and awareness by showing a growth in thought and experiences over time. However, necessarily, as I am writing this book now, it is through the lens of the current universe that I see.

I studied with Rikka Zimmerman for five years. I was in her coaching program that lasted two years. I am a certified coach in her Life Transformed Coaching program. I have her permission to share her teachings.

I have changed the names of friends and acquaintances, so that they can maintain their privacy. I didn't change the name of family members; they know who they are. I have left the names of individuals who are in the profession of spirituality, since they want to be seen and heard. They are also listed in the back of the book as resources.

Animals have played an important role in my life, as both friend and teacher. I close each chapter with the mention of an animal that I believe represents that chapter's path.

Feel free to read this book in any order. It doesn't really make a difference where you start. All paths, like spokes on a wheel, head inward, to the center of our being. Some roads just take longer than others. This book is a culmination of my four-year exploration with spirituality.

If I had to summarize this book into a singular idea, it would be: *God's love is all there is.* I came to this realization through the experience of joy, and without the grief and loss that I experienced, I never would have found Joy. The incidents in our lives are really in divine perfection, and if we only willing to let go of struggle, we would know it. Health, wealth, and wisdom are mere dances in that divine perfection. If you already know this, you probably won't learn anything from this book—but you just might enjoy my recounting of it anyway.

FULL CIRCLE

On August 22, 2012, I had a reading with Asia Voight, an animal communicator with whom I had been studying animal communication. She said that I would/should go to the Bahamian island of Bimini and experience the great wall of Atlantis; to be in the high-frequency vibrations of that place and swim in 20–40 feet of water. On February 15, 2016, almost four years later, I swam over the Atlantis Road in Bimini, in 20–40 feet of water. I experienced many powerful visions of high energy.

At the time that I spoke with Asia, I didn't even know that Bimini existed. And when I was there I didn't remember my conversation with Asia. But in the process of writing this book, many experiences and thoughts have come together in a similar way for me. This book shares many of these experiences.

I wrote this book for me, so that I may know who I truly am. And I hope that in the unfolding of my journey, you may come to a better knowing of yourself. I hope that you will laugh, love, and cry as you read it—because that is what I did as I wrote it.

MORNING PRAYER

Morning Prayer is how I begin all of my mornings. I have done so for many years. The formalization of this prayer began in Bimini, but it had many less formalized predecessors before that. This prayer was inspired by St. Francis of Assisi's prayer: "Let me be an instrument of thy peace."

My prayer goes beyond being a vessel, as I already know that I am one. So I am really asking that I may notice how much I am a vessel in any given moment of the day. And is there even more than that? My surroundings are just a reflection of the state I am in—so noticing them is just noticing myself.

Today's word is "truth." So how much truth do I see reflected back at me, and where do I see it? The day is early and we shall see.

My Morning Prayer currently goes like this:

> *Thank you, God, for this beautiful day. Thank you. Thank you. Thank you for this wonderful place we live. Thank you for the plants and animals that share our lives with us. And today for the wonderful fire in the fireplace.*
>
> *Make me an instrument of thy peace, love, joy, beauty, harmony, grace, healing, communication, abundance, gratitude, magic, bliss, truth, divine perfection, and cocreation. What shall I notice today?*
>
> *What shall I be so much of that everything reflects back to me; so much that I stand in awe of my own being? I listen. And I hear, Truth. Today my word is "truth."*

I start with gratitude for the day and for all things. The deeper I go into gratitude, the greater the experience becomes. I know that all magic starts with the catalyst of gratitude. No matter what the day looks like. A gorgeous sunrise makes it easy to be thankful. So I usually start there, because it is easy.

Often, it is rainy, cloudy, cold, or windy. I am still grateful. Today it is four degrees below zero. I am grateful. I am grateful to be sitting in front of the fireplace, warmed by the glow of the embers, writing this book. So that is my morning prayer.

I have tried to capture the significant events and memories of these last few years. Many of them happened before my Joy experience, in Bimini; I formalized them in a big way after that. There were also many previous experiences that were formative but not necessarily spiritual in nature, such as the Marshall Islands, Samoa, and Europe. I have also included a few experiences that were simply funny, or in some way exemplary of an idea.

How is it that a life is both ordinary and extraordinary at the same time?

A friend gave me a thank-you card. It said: "My friends called me delusional. I laughed so hard I almost fell off my unicorn." I think that would be a good name for my book: *My Spiritual Name Is Falling Off Unicorns, Laughing.* This is what my spirit would name it.

But I will call it *From Heartache to Joy,* because I think that people want to let go of their sadness and grief, and want to live in joy. Although what these people really need to do is to fall off their unicorns, laughing—they just don't know it yet.

This is not meant to be a how-to book. Each of us must find our own way. But I have put the processes and exercises at the end of each chapter and all together in the last chapter, so that those of you who wish to try them can easily do so. I have also included a reference list of the individuals, websites, and books that I have mentioned, so that you may experience their ideas directly for yourself.

CHAPTER 1

Access Love
Go Through Fear

"Choose your power, not your fear.
We are all one, but different."

—Asia Voight

It was Easter and he was several hours late.

I was at a friend's house for Easter dinner and John, my husband, was to show up for dinner with the horse trailer, having delivered two mares to the nearby Wisconsin Equine Clinic for artificial insemination. As the horse trailer would not fit on the narrow driveway of my friend's home, we had called the police to get permission to park it close by on another street.

It was nine pm, and I was tired of worrying. What if he was in an accident? What if something had happened to the mares? *What if... What if...* I had been pacing for an hour.

Finally, around ten, he arrived, parked the trailer, and everything was fine.

That night I became very sick. I was feverish and had diarrhea. I ran to the bathroom so many times, I had nothing left inside me.

I was sick for the next three days. I didn't eat anything. People said that I had the flu, but I knew that I was clearing out all the poison the anxiety had left in my body. I had worried myself sick. Anxiety makes us sick, literally—and it isn't even real. We tell ourselves a story, and in the retelling, over and over, we make it more real. And then we lock it in place.

That was my lesson. And I learned it.

MOVING THROUGH FEAR

Why do I put fear front and center in a chapter on accessing love? Because we have to feel and move through fear to get to love.

Is fear really a polarity of love? It can be seen as that. But true Love has no polarity.

What *is* fear? Is it even real? It *feels* real. So fear is a feeling. Why do we care about it?

We care because fear stops us from moving forward and taking action. It locks us into the status quo.

> *Love your fear into harmony so it can't come back home with you.*

Your heart races, your breathing is fast. You tell yourself it's fear. If you believe that it's fear, then that's what you get. If you believe it's painful, then that's what you get.

It's just energy. Expand yourself out: the fear disappears. If it disappears that easily, how real was it to begin with?

Open yourself up bigger. Expand out and move beyond the fear. Be bigger and breathe. Look at all of it. It is just energy.

Energy won't kill you. You are the energy that you feel.

Try delivering the whole story about fear into a bubble. Then blow the bubble away—send the bubble with the fear and anxiety in it out into the universe with your breath. Release fear back to where it came from. It wasn't even yours to begin with. It just floats out there in the environment, and you let it in. Let it go.

THE FEAR SHOWDOWN

The year is 2013 and I am having a showdown with fear. We are in front of the OK Corral and our weapons are drawn. My weapon is love and light. Fear's weapon is a stun gun. When we banish fear with love, we reclaim the power to act. We let go of forcing and pushing. When we let go of fear, we can reach for higher levels of love. The universe is always returning us to love. Tell fear, "I know that you are love and light." The fear dissipates into the energy of love.

Choose your thoughts for their emotional content, and then stay in that place. Make peace with where you are. Let go of the resistance. Feel the fear, and then reach through it to something else. Find something to feel good about and then get out of the way. Honor yourself by choosing what feels light, expansive, and joyful.

Choose yes instead of no. The universe is continually expanding. It only understands yes. Find ways to say yes so that the universe can hear you.

What if fear is your energetic power? If so, relax into it. Let go of your resistance to fear. When you undefine your fear, it dissolves, like sugar in water. Allow your fear to be exciting. Take fear and play with it—for one minute or two minutes. Be brave. Then allow what the fear is there to teach you to come through. Listen and take inspired action.

Energy won't kill you. You are the energy that you feel. Then you expand into it.

MUD AROUND MY ANKLES

Can we allow ourselves to see without our eyes? What sees when we dream? It's not our eyes.

Several years ago I had a dream that I was confronted by three-foot-deep mud I had to wade through. It came to me that I could use an elephant to pull me through the mud. But then I thought about the elephant getting stuck and decided to just walk through, pushing my feet along the bottom. When I got to the other side I looked down at my boots: They were brown suede with fur. They were also perfectly clean and had no mud.

These boots were made for walkin' and that's just what I'll do. Ha!

Let go of the fear; play with it. Reality tries to grab at your ankles and hold you in the mud. Keep looking up. Notice it, expect it, but don't project it. Just notice it. Are you willing to be comfortable with the uncomfortable? Are you willing to really feel fear? Knock down "I don't know" so that you can function in the world of knowing.

In 2014 I watched a YouTube video by Ester Hicks on worry. In it, she said and I paraphrase:

> *Wait until you are in alignment before you take action. Make a decision and then line up with it. Feel inspiration. Don't line up with 'I should.' Shift yourself from worry. The more you worry, the more the worries come. Shift away from the worry and they will go away. The universe hears what you mean and not what you say. If you have a negative emotion and don't deal with it, you get sick. Ease while you are working is better than stress while you are working.*

> —ESTER HICKS

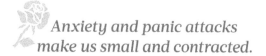

Anxiety and panic attacks make us small and contracted.

CONTROL FREAK

Sometimes we try to use control to knock down fear. When the control freak shows up, no amount of information will make it go away. Embrace your inner control freak until it disappears. Come back to the breath. Don't judge it.

Is it fear that is coming up, or is it fear that is leaving? Fear is coming up just to leave again.

Whatever we think we want for someone else, we really want for ourselves. If we get stuck trying to change others, we should ask: What am I trying to get from this? And then we should give it to ourselves first. Whatever we are trying to give or get for ourselves—we already have it. We don't have to give or get it. We can rest in knowing that we already have it.

When others try to control you, don't believe in it. Eventually they give up when you don't believe in their control.

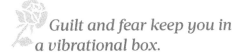 *Guilt and fear keep you in a vibrational box.*

HENRIETTA AND CONTROL

I have a very loving, giving, and courageous shirttail relative you could call a control freak. Her name is Henrietta and her kids and family certainly call her a control freak.

If you are in her house and she asks you a question, she's gone before you can answer it—to some urgent issue in some other part of the house. She is full of angst and conspiracy theories. There is a lot of justification for it in her story, because she came here from an Eastern European country, fleeing oppression and death.

Henrietta will follow you around, asking, "Can I bring you water? Tea? Anything?" The hovering is constant. While she is very generous and loving, there is no breath or space. The need to control is just behind her generosity.

Henrietta called me the other night. She was, as usual sad, angry, and frustrated—for good reason. She was sure that I too was sad and that something was wrong in my life. She kept asking, "Are you sure you are okay? Are you sure?" She is dedicated to being sure that we are not okay, and will not stop asking until she has determined that it is so.

But I now realize that this behavior is just an aspect of her need for control. She is trying to control us with her angst and sadness. She is only content when she believes she is in control. But there's no such thing as control, really. It's a losing game.

I do my best to smile at her sadness. I know that joy is a choice, and also we must each find our own way. Some people *have* to struggle; it's the only way they can feel worthy. They believe that pain and struggle will get them to God. Many religions teach this.

I believe that heaven is already here on earth, and that we are meant to live in joy as well as in all experiences. We have the choice to take a direction, but we have no control. I beam the joy of my being out at Henrietta and out at all others. I wait with patience for God to lighten her load when she is ready to let go of her need to struggle.

THE DANCE WITH FEAR

What if fear is just a partner that we dance with? *Fear, would you like to tango?* I dance with fear of snakes. I am afraid of snakes. Many people are, so this is a good example.

Generally, when I see a snake, I am airborne. I jump when one is near, and in the air I look down and say, "Why am I in the air?" Part of me is not really afraid. But I still jump into the air anyway. By the time I reach the ground, I am no longer afraid. But I leave the area, and don't go near that spot again for a few hours.

I have had several run-ins with snakes.

If you fear it, it will come.

 *We try to give birth to fear to clear it.*

John and I went hiking in a nature preserve. We were picking mushrooms, and I wondered if we would encounter any snakes. Of course, as soon as I began wondering this, we did. We saw more snakes on that trip than my husband had seen in his entire life.

He, of course, has no fear of snakes. He carried them around in his shirt when he was young. He and his brothers used to torture their mom by bringing them to the dinner table hidden in their shirts. They just sat there giggling until his mom said, "Okay, what have you got in your shirt?"

On the other hand…

I have let the serpent climb my spine and look out through my head. I look out. And we dance. We undulate. We dance the dance of fear.

I create my own fear and I dance with it. Why? Because it is more interesting than dancing alone. Because it reminds me that I am alive. I don't let it paralyze me. Then it would not be a dance. I would be a stone statue, stunned by the gun of fear.

What if fear is there so that we can dance with tension and feel alive? What if fear is just excitement?

I have to let go of my resistance to the fear of snakes. If I don't, they will keep showing up until I do. The universe doesn't respond to no. It doesn't respond to *I hope there are no snakes here*. The universe only responds to yes. Yes, I will dance the dance that presents itself. And I choose to dance with butterflies over here.

Perhaps we just dance with fear, until the music stops.

FEAR IS NOT IN THE PRESENT

In 2015 I begin to play with the idea that fear and anxiety exist in the past and future but not in the present moment. Anxiety is about something that might happen in the future. "What if" is in the future. Fear, on the other hand, is based on a past experience. In a way fear is made up. It isn't real. Fear can be in the present moment if a bear is chasing you in the woods. That experience is fear that isn't made up. If we exist in the present moment, then we don't step in the fear poop.

In 2016 I turned the subject of fear toward my horsemanship. The human-horse partnership is a great example of how love penetrates fear.

Fear and anxiety are prevalent in the horse world. It is the love of the horse that makes people persevere through their fear. When riding in a clinic, you are generally asked, on a scale of 1–10, where are you in your emotional maturity? What is your horse's emotional maturity? If you are a 5 and your horse is a 5, you are probably okay together. If your horse is a 2 and you are a 2—well, there may be some black and blue in your future.

In traditional horsemanship, the horse is seen as a tool and the person is the boss, there to tell the tool what to do. In natural horsemanship, the horse is our partner. We try to create situations in which our idea becomes the horse's idea, and then together we execute that idea to the best of our abilities, using equal doses of *love, language, and leadership.*

Fear and anxiety enter in because we need caution, and awareness, as well as some knowledge of horse behavior. The more we know and the more tools we have, the less fearful we can become.

Anxiety is different from fear. One of my trainers calls anxiety "made-up fear." It's not real. It's something that we worry about that *might* happen in the future. I call it "anticipatory anxiety." Anxiety can cause things to happen—just like with the snakes. If you are afraid of falling off and you are looking at the ground, then that is likely where you will end up.

> *Calmness is in the present moment.*

Horses are aware of our feelings. They mirror us, as do many animals. If we are anxious, then they become anxious. Then we become more anxious, they become more anxious. It is a dangerous circle that you don't want to get sucked into.

Horses are prey animals. Humans are predators. When they are afraid, they run off. When we are afraid, we clench our muscles, which feels like an attack to the horse. So he runs off.

Calm and at ease is where you want to be. Riding can be delightful as a breeze and exhilarating as the wind. And it can go bad in an instant. Awareness, knowledge, and calm are where you need to be when you are with your horse. Knowing this can put tension on the top of calm, on top of what may have already been fear. You have to let it all go and just be in the present with the horse, who is always in the present moment.

Horses teach us to be in the present moment. Neither fear nor anxiety exists in the present moment.

Over the last thirty years, I have been bucked off horses, trampled by them, and have broken my wrist. Most people who ride horses have broken some bone or other (often the collarbone). But my apprehension and anxiety around horses is not about me: it's about them.

Remember, anxiety is just made up. It doesn't exist in the present, and yet we can make ourselves sick, as in when my husband got back late with the trailer. The event happened, but the emotion is made-up. How we feel about it is a choice.

It is very easy to make up a story about why we are afraid. *The last time I did this, this happened; it might happen again. It's too hot or too cold or too windy. My horse is too...* The story itself isn't the problem. We have the choice to arm ourselves with knowledge, awareness, and love. We have the choice to stay in the present moment. It's the only place that exists anyway. And in this moment we are safe.

COMFORT ZONE

I tell myself that I don't have to try anything that I don't want to do. Then I do what is in my comfort zone, and then I sometimes think, *Well, maybe I'll just try this....* And I surprise myself at how easy it was. And then maybe I try something else—and then go back into my comfort zone. I just move closer and stay longer. There is a book out there by that title, *Move Closer and Stay Longer* by Stephanie Burns. It helped me see a way to step out of my comfort zone—to be comfortably uncomfortable.

> *"Move closer and stay longer."*
> —STEPHANIE BURNS

My husband had a sticker on the refrigerator for a long time. It said, "Worry is like sitting in rocking chair. There is a whole lot of motion, but you don't get anywhere."

Worry is a waste of time. We put the label of fear or anxiety on the energy moving through us. Why not put a different label on it and call it "excitement" or "joy?" Sit, stand, and act in love. Love contains all things, including the made-up feelings of anxiety and fear.

> *When you point yourself at fear, it can be dissolved with love. When you point yourself at love, fear doesn't exist.*

Exercises to Go Through Fear

1. Place your anxiety or fear into a bubble and blow it away. Do this literally or figuratively.

2. Go where you don't want to go. Enter your fear or anxiety. Go there and feel it for ninety seconds, until it dissipates.

3. Enter the edge of your comfort zone. Approach and retreat. Approach and retreat. Until you have a new edge.

The **Spider** *spins his web.*

CHAPTER 2

Allow Love

Yesterday, my husband told me that he loved love. We were watching a chick flick on TV, and when the two love interests kissed, he sighed and said, "I just love love." He thought about it some more, and said, "I just love love!" And he gave me that look that melted my heart more than fifty years ago.

Isn't that an interesting turn of phrase: "melted my heart?" It isn't our heart that melts. It's the resistance to love that we carry around, to protect us from being hurt, that melts. The resistance melts in the presence of love. It *feels* like our heart melts. But actually love is just shining through.

 *Love is more than a feeling.*

It was always there. Our minds were just trying to protect us by resisting it.

We don't need that protection. Tell your mind: "It's okay, mind. I've got this. You can let go now and go play elsewhere for a while. Go amuse yourself." I give my mind details to play with and then I am free to feel and be love.

So what is love? How do we get into love? How do we stay in love? *Can* one stay in love? What does love feel like? Is true love different from God's Love—or different from what we mean when we say that we love someone or something?

NO QUESTIONS

It's 2013 and I tell myself that questions take me out of my present-moment awareness. Questions take me out of love.

I don't care about how, or why. My job is to be myself. I cannot heal or change anyone else.

LOVE IS ALL THERE IS

My first live experience with Rikka Zimmerman and Zach Rehder was in Chicago in 2013. I took a break from taking care of my mom, attended a class, then came back to Mom's house, where I wrote the following.

> *What do I know now that I did not know before? I know that my headaches are requesting me to be in the present moment and that they cannot exist in that moment. All pain disappears in the present moment. And with practice it is possible to reside in that moment.*
>
> *I know that a flower is here to tell me that I am beautiful when I walk by. And to tell me that it loves me. I thought that I was here to tell it that it is beautiful. I know that a manmade chair is also beautiful and that the chair has a purpose. That purpose is to provide me comfort and to love me back, so that I may know that I walk in the grace of God with love.*
>
> *I'm reminded of the Beatles song "All You Need Is Love." I thought that there was no way for any part of that song to not be true. All parts are true in and of themselves.*
>
> *All you need is love.*
> *All*
> *All you*
> *All you need*
> *All you need is*
> *All you need is love.*

DIVINE RELATIONSHIPS

A year later, in February 2014, I was listening to a webinar by Rikka, about relationships. She said that hanging on to being right is more important to some people than being loved. The following is a paraphrase from that webinar.

> *Enjoy the energy of a divine relationship. Allow and live the energy of divine relationship. Nothing has to be different for the world to love you infinitely. Bring in the future of that beautiful divine relationship. You don't have to be perfect or earn your way. You just have to say yes and allow. If you don't love yourself, it might be because you don't want to validate that 'they' should have loved you. You are hanging on to being right about them not loving you. Me being loved is more important than hanging on to anything.*
>
> —RIKKA ZIMMERMAN

THE ACT OF BECOMING

A while back, I noticed that:

I hate Hate.

I love Love.

I fear Fear.

I enjoy Joy.

This awareness felt true for where I was at in my spiritual growth. But I wasn't sure what it meant.

I now believe that it was the act of becoming—of moving into being what you feel. If you hate Hate, you are becoming it. If you love Love, you are becoming Love. I knew that I had to let go of hating Hate, but it took me until 2015 to realize that I needed to love hate to dissolve it.

 *Emotion is love in motion.*

PRAISE AND SELF-WORTH

In April of 2014, I took a Self-Love Mastery Course from Rikka. She told a story of her own reactions to praise, and how they relate to self-worth.

When people swarm up after a performance and say, 'I love you. You are so wonderful,' I don't react. Or I say 'thank you.' Also inside of that is their own 'I am not so wonderful, and I could never do that.' What the performer receives is the praise and the 'I am not deserving.' The result of this is, I didn't do very well and they are lying. Unless you believe that you are wonderful without the praise, their own undeserving is thrust at you and you receive it as if it were your own.

—RIKKA ZIMMERMAN

My own experience with receiving praise has always been interesting. Many years ago, when I was in my twenties and about to leave the country, I received an award from the Business and Professional Woman's club for Outstanding Woman of the Year. I was the current president and was about to leave my position.

It was a total surprise. Another club decided to give me the same award also—though I was not a member of that club, and hadn't even heard of it. They just jumped on the bandwagon.

I felt I didn't deserve the awards and that they really had nothing to do with me—which they didn't. They had more to do with those giving the awards and what they needed, not what I needed, or deserved. I was pleased, however, to be recognized.

Fast forward to twenty-five years later and I was teaching at a college. At that time, I would have very much liked to receive the outstanding teacher award, but I never did. All my colleagues around me received it, but not me.

It wasn't that I didn't deserve it. I was, in fact, an excellent teacher. It was that I wanted/needed it. When we want or need something, it has a tendency to not show up. *Neediness* is a place where we get our buttons pushed.

Acceptance is just saying to yourself, *This happened.* And not aligning with right or wrong, but just getting to the space of neutrality. *This is neither right nor wrong. It just is.*

ELIMINATING CONDITIONAL CARING

Caring sometimes looks like wanting something for someone else. Many people on a spiritual path have an abundance of caring, which often comes with judgment, resentment, and repressed anger. Judgment keeps you wanting people to behave in a certain way.

The energy of love is so far beyond what we usually think of as loving. But we can choose to go around the cognitive mind, the "should"s of caring, and embody the energetic field. Every definition is a way that our world tries to control us into being the same. Our mind does this to keep us safe.

Go around it: embody the infinite and the unknown. True love goes beyond conditional caring.

RELEASING IS FORGIVING

I now realize that forgiving myself for the "wrongdoings" I have played as perpetrator also releases the victims from their victimhood. When we forgive, we release the energy stuck in place. I didn't know that I was keeping them in victimhood by maintaining my ties to an event. The act of releasing myself also releases them. Of course, their releasing themselves as victim also releases me as perpetrator. Hanging on to any of it protects no one. Letting go protects everyone. Letting go is just one "d" away from letting God.

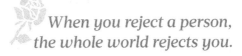

When you reject a person,
the whole world rejects you.

THE INVISIBLE BRIDGE

In August 2015, I was listening to Jennifer Mclean on Healing with the Masters. She was interviewing a guest about being rescued by an invisible angel.

What stayed in my mind was the mention of falling out onto a bridge. In my mind this was like a scene in one of the *Indiana Jones* series. The bridge was hidden but Indiana Jones just stepped out onto it as if he knew it was there. And, of course, he was saved, for the moment.

Within the hour, I heard the same bridge reference, on a replay from Rikka's Vib class, a weekly membership class. *Hmm.* My question from the class the week before had been about letting go of control and falling into the hands of God. The question was, how do I do that?

Trusting and stepping out onto the bridge—that was my answer. We need to trust that the bridge of God is there to support us. Because it is.

FALLING INTO LOVE

Why do we say falling *in* love? We trust falling into love, like stepping out onto the bridge. It's all about allowing.

Allowing the power of God/Love to flow through you without stopping it is about being an empty vessel so that there is room for it to flow through you.

But we have free will. We can go elsewhere. The world is constantly changing in vibration. What we consider to be a higher vibration today will be just normal tomorrow. Today's vibration is higher than yesterday. So we have only now to consider. What is the vibration right now, right here?

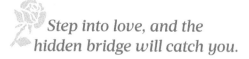 *Step into love, and the hidden bridge will catch you.*

RESISTING AND EMBRACING FEAR

I have been noticing my resistance more and more. In a webinar I was listening to, a person called in complaining about access to the class. I resisted the anger and frustration of the person; I judged them. I didn't know yet that I had the same anger and frustration inside of me. On a recorded "call-in" with Rikka, she said "Embrace your fear." Since I carry a great deal of fear and anticipatory anxiety, I was listening closely. I always "try" to embrace my fear. But what does that really mean and what does it really look like? How do I do that? What does it feel like to embrace your fear?

Then I thought about my "fearing fear" and "loving love." I realized in that moment: the verb creates the noun. Loving actually creates love. Love responds to or reacts to loving. I also realized that when we love fear, fear has no option but to turn into love. It's that simple. That easy.

So, when I love me, I have no choice but to be love, and in fact, I already am love. I loved my headache, it went away. I loved my stomachache, it went away. Not that something else isn't coming up; it always will. Then we have to love that too. If you are a chronic pain sufferer, see Chapter 11: Heal with Love.

Being all energy is infinite love.

JUDGMENT, HATE, AND ANGER

What if we let go of our belief in cause and effect? When a person stubs their toe, it hurts. Or at least it seems to. But what if something else entirely is going on?

That is a simple event. When we talk about complex events, like people growing up with caretakers who abuse them, and continuing or not continuing the perpetration of the abuse, or even something as complex as war, cause and effect go out the window. Because who really knows why people do the things they do?

It feels good to live in love. It doesn't feel good to live in hate and anger. Anger motivates you to action—but you still have a choice. You can choose to do what returns you to love.

I think it's about the movement of energy. Without hate and anger, we might not get off the couch to do anything about anything. Sitting on the couch is not the answer. Energy has to move. Moving and doing is flowing with the energy naturally. Judgment, on the other hand, resists that flow. Judgment becomes a rock in the water.

"Why" and "how" are judgments. Knowing that all things return to God precludes any need to know why and how we behave. If you go around the rock and continue with the flow, you get returned to God sooner. As if sooner exists; as if the journey itself is not the real flow of energy moving in love.

I give up trying to understand. I allow and let God.

I busy my mind with the details. I allow my heart to sit in love and let my mind think that it is creating love through understanding. It's just busy-bee work. BZZZZ. The mind is trying to take credit for the love that already exists in the heart.

We can let go of identity: feel the "I don't know."

We can allow the soul to inform every aspect of our reality—and unravel, from a being of personality to a being of spirit. The unraveling empowers us. If we are vibrating out infinite possibility, then the loop will return back to us.

Support is what is required. Acceptance and divine love support you. These two work together. If you can't love what happens, you can just feel it and be with it. It is the holding on that feeds your identity. Identity is not wrong or bad; it just gets in the way. We are already perfect. We can just swim in the ocean of oneness.

I am grateful to be right here right now. I let go of the fear of "I don't know." A part of me permanently lives in the "I don't know." She enjoys the freedom of it. She doesn't need to know. Questions take you out of present-moment awareness.

 *Source your awareness.*

FEEL THE HURT

How do I really feel about a painful event? I feel hurt. What can I do for the benefit of my inner child, my little one? My little one doesn't trust me to keep her safe.

I go to the mirror and tell her that I love her when her heart is cracked open.

It is hard to see hurt as a gift. But hurt is like an alarm clock that reminds us to open our hearts to more love.

Thank God for the alarm going off. Thank the hurt for hurting. Love the hurt. Then guess what? It disappears. It doesn't hurt anymore. Love melts hurt away. Love is beneath all things.

Allow your heart to break. Allow it to break so deeply that it opens to everything.

GIFT OF LOVE

Love is being in a divine relationship with God. Life is the gift of watching God breathe his love into us. With every breath, we breathe in the exhale of God's love. With our exhale, God breathes in our experiences, which are his gift of life to us.

I do not know who I am or where I am going. But I trust in God's love to support me with the unseen bridge. I allow the heart/mind to navigate joyously and safely through the mine fields of reality. True love contains all things, all the chapters in this book and all the chapters in all the books that ever were and ever will be written. We call it unconditional love because it exists, no matter what, when, why, how much, or how often. Love just is.

In high school I had to memorize Elizabeth Barrett Browning's poem "How Do I Love Thee."

> *How do I love thee? Let me count the ways.*
> *I love thee to the depth and breadth and height*
> *My soul can reach, when feeling out of sight*
> *For the ends of being and ideal grace.*
> *I love thee to the level of every day's*
> *Most quiet need, by sun and candle-light.*
> *I love thee freely, as men strive for right.*
> *I love thee purely, as they turn from praise.*
> *I love thee with the passion put to use*
> *In my old griefs, and with my childhood's faith.*
> *I love thee with a love I seemed to lose*
> *With my lost saints. I love thee with the breath,*
> *Smiles, tears, of all my life; and, if God choose,*
> *I shall but love thee better after death.*

How is it that she said all of these things in so few words so long ago? Why is it that it takes me so many words?

Exercises for Allowing Love

1. Mirror work.

   Look into a mirror and tell your little one what s/he needs to hear. Ask her, "What do you need to hear about this?" Listen. And then tell her what she needs to hear. The answer will be something like: "I love you. I will keep you safe. You are beautiful." Look into your left eye in the mirror and tell her what she needs to hear.

2. Morning Prayer.

   Say whatever prayer you like and end with: "God, how much Love can I possibly be today? Show me how much Love I am. Show me how much you Love me." And then feel, listen, and watch.

The **Dog** *wags his tail in unconditional love.*

CHAPTER 3

The Way of Peace

Use Anger and Frustration

THE WAFFLE

I was sitting at breakfast one morning, about halfway through a weeklong Life Transformed Coach's training in Bimini. We had eaten egg whites and what the locals considered to be "healthy food" for several days. There was also oatmeal, good fresh fruit, and the same bran muffin every day.

When we arrived at the buffet table on this particular morning, there was something new: waffles. While many of the participants were gluten-free, others, myself included, were very happy to see the waffles. They looked to be previously frozen or packaged—but hey, they were still waffles!

I sat down to enjoy my fresh fruit, coffee, and waffle. I started to cut into it, but it was extremely tough. There was no cutting it, even with a knife. I gave up trying and picked it up to eat it. It tasted okay, but not as satisfying as I had expected.

Other people began to join me at the table. One woman sat across from me and started to try to cut her waffle with her knife. She grunted and groaned, and still kept trying to cut it. I watched as she struggled with it, and finally I said to her, "You don't have to struggle, you know. You can just pick it up."

She thought about it, and said, "I'll just keep at it a little longer."

I waited, continued eating, and after a couple minutes more I asked her, "Are you ready to let go of your struggle yet?"

She said, "I'll just try a little longer."

A little while later she stopped, put down her knife and fork, and looked at me. Then we both broke out laughing.

She had chosen to keep struggling—even though she knew she was struggling, and that there was an easier way. What a great metaphor for life. *I'll just struggle a little longer.* Ha!

What are struggle, frustration, anger, and overwhelm? Why do we feel them? Is it bad or wrong to feel them? Are they the polarities of peace? What is peace? Are anger and rage bad feelings? Why is it so hard to be in the face of rage?

USE ANGER AND FRUSTRATION

Anger can be a useful motivator, and struggle is just a matter of perspective. When we fully experience anger and frustration, we can find the peace that is on the other side.

There is a hierarchy of emotions, and understanding them is useful in learning to take small steps. This chapter offers many exercises for releasing frustration and using anger.

> *When you take the content out of anger and just be with it, you see that it is just energy.*

ANGER AND RAGE

We need to play with our intense energies. Move into the resistance.

Anger is the ego's refusal to trust in the soul's journey. Ask yourself, What am I trying to prove to myself about this? Don't judge your feelings. Feel them. Judging yourself for having them just keeps you stuck.

Allow the frequencies to flow through you. Use the energy of anger to eliminate the limitation you have created around yourself. Use rage, and throw it at limitation.

If someone tells you that you can't do something, and you get angry, you might feel boxed in. What if you threw your anger at the box? Boom! The box is gone. Now you are free to choose to do the activity or not—and to do it without the blindness that anger causes. Getting angry at the other person, or at yourself, or repressing it is not helpful. So release your anger at the box, which is limitation. One way to do this is to go outside. Sit in nature. Scream at a tree. The tree won't mind. Or sit in your car and yell at your windshield.

Let go of everything. Celebrate feeling it, like a little child. Small children express their feelings until they are taught not to.

> *Feeling is the experience of energy through judgment.*

JUDGMENT

Judgment, too, is just energy. When you are no longer affected by judgment, you can embody the feeling so fully that it just is. Feel the feeling, and graciously hand the world back to itself. When you take the content out of anger and can just be with it, you see that it is just energy. Whatever you react to is the content. Everything that is occurring is getting energy up and out.

RESPONSIBILITY

I ask myself, What am I ready to let go of? All responsibility? Once I let go of responsibility, then responsibility becomes fun. It is no longer a burden. Falling off the unicorn is my responsibility. Or not falling off, as the case may be. John has a T-shirt that says, "My Indian Name Is Falling Off Horses." It is his responsibility to not fall off. I should have a T-shirt that says, "My Spiritual Name Is Falls off Unicorns, Laughing." Now that's a responsibility that I can hang out with. Falling off or not falling off, and doing it while laughing is my responsibility.

Your resistance is to the intensity of the feeling. *Oh, well, it's just a human experience.* What if you could have a human body and not suffer a human experience? What would you need to know?

You are creating the bread crumbs to lead you back home. What if the feelings of your experiences were like the bread crumbs of Hansel and Gretel? And what if each one led you back home to God and yourself? What if they led to Peace? Can you allow yourself to be excited? Lean into your anger, or your joy. Why do we own anger more than we own joy, or awesomeness? You can't hurt people with love. End the struggle with anger and frustration, and there is no fight. There is no conflict. Identity and spirit want to be free.

Our stories about our emotions lock the emotions in place. Let go of the story and you let go of the emotion.

IDENTITY AND REFERENCE POINTS

It is good to not have any reference points. When we let go of our identity, we lose our reference points. When we lose our reference points, we are aligned with ourselves. Then, when you are with a person who makes you unhappy, you can ask, what are they bringing up in me? What are they projecting onto me? Fear holds the sadness in place. The need for perfection keeps you from receiving. Embrace the letting go of identity and you can live in absolute freedom and peace in every moment. Your soul's goal is to have an outrageously good time.

Care more about love than about being right.

STRUGGLE

We have engaged struggle as if it were a computer program that we're running on ourselves.

> *Is pain something you set up to make sure you come home? Sometimes we need to have the worst-case scenarios happen. Or could we just be nudged lovingly along? 'If everything was perfect, would you have bought this program?' Would you choose more consciousness? If you had perfect health, perfect money, perfect love, what would you seek? What if every choice, such as money, was the perfect choice?*
> —RIKKA ZIMMERMAN

If everything was perfect, would you have bought this book? If everything was perfect, I would still seek more fun and more power. What if struggle is just the next step in my evolution, to move me into light and love? I don't need to have pain in order to choose them.

24

Nudge me lightly. I am listening now.

You don't have to experience anything in order to receive love. Let go of struggle, and let go of trying to trust—try instead to just know it. As a child and young person, I watched my mother struggle to provide for us. (Although it wasn't all struggle—there were many marvelous and wondrous adventures also.) Watching her struggle, I decided not to struggle. I decided not to try to do it all. Not to try to have a career and raise a family. The doctors told my mother if she didn't slow down she wouldn't live long enough to see us graduate from high school. I heard that and made my decision not to have children.

THE HIERARCHY OF EMOTIONS

I was visiting a friend in San Francisco early in the summer of 2015, and I picked up a book from their bookshelf: *The Law of Attraction* by Ester and Jerry Hicks. I read it that morning while my friend was at work. What stuck in my mind as important at that time was the *Hierarchy of Emotions*. The theory was new to me. It helped me to better understand John, my husband, and Jeremy, my brother. The idea that anger is higher and feels better than depression or fear; that blame is higher than anger; that worry is higher than blame. Counselors can lead people out of their anger only to put them back into their depression.

Depression is inward and doesn't usually affect those around us. Anger is directed outward and is more uncomfortable to those around us. This was an interesting idea for me. Those feelings that we usually think of as higher emotions, like hope, optimism, enthusiasm, passion, joy, love, and freedom are at the top of the hierarchy. It is too hard to go from depression to Joy. It's easier to take little steps, smaller emotional jumps, through anger, revenge, overwhelm, and contentment. Here we are taking little steps again.

If they don't do what we want, we think that they have done something wrong.

My husband, John, gets angry at everything. He stubs his toe, he is angry. We laugh, and I call him a pirate.

"Aaaarg," he says. I say "Aaaarg" back at him and he laughs.

He uses anger to motivate himself. He wants to fix everything. He is a high J (judgmental) on the MMPS (the Minnesota Multiphasic Personality Inventory, used to assess adult psychopathology). I am most effective from a state of peace or calm. I can't function when I am depressed. I can't even move off the couch. I function best from Joy.

John uses anger to get his butt up off the couch. He hates "admiring the problem" and just wants to fix it. He doesn't complain about the weather or complain just to complain. He gets angry, and then takes action.

It can be difficult to be in the face of anger. Rage is even more difficult. If you resist it in yourself, it is even more difficult to be in its presence. If you don't resist it, it becomes easier to be around.

I love complaining about the weather. It feels good to complain. I have red hair and get fiery mad. I flash in an instant, and almost as soon as I have flashed, it is gone. I don't hold on to it. I just think, *Well, that felt good.* I allow myself to get mad, and to express it. Then it's gone.

> *Holding the feeling in is what causes us to feel pain and get sick.*

I used to judge John for his anger. While I still feel uncomfortable around it, I now realize that it is just a step in the hierarchy of emotions. It's better than depression or being numb on the couch.

Anger is his motivator. He has very big energy, but he is careful to not direct it at anyone. He tends to go outside and yell at the trees or the snow or some dumb inanimate object like a hammer that just hit his thumb. "Aaaarg," he says. And we laugh.

LITTLE BY LITTLE

I used to judge others for their blame and their refusal to take responsibility for their lives. I thought they should just choose happiness, responsibility, and peace. But now I realize that blame is a higher order than anger, and that worry is even higher than blame. So blame is just their way of working out of their emotional trauma, step by step.

Awareness is just observing, not trying to fix or change, or wish that the other would change. It is a state of allowing. Judging is wishing that they were different.

Learning that emotions are or can be stepping stones for other emotions helped me to get out of judgment around certain emotional states of being—the negative ones, like anger, rage, overwhelm, and fear.

Of all people, I should realize the value of emotional stepping stones. I love taking little steps. I take life's challenges in small pieces. I used to grade drawings: five drawings a day. I play with my horse: one hour every day. I write in my journal: five pages a day. I meditate: every morning for one hour. That is how I set forth in my tasks, a little bit at a time.

BILLY FINGERS AND JEREMY

While visiting the same friend in San Francisco, I picked up a second book: *The Afterlife of Billy Fingers* by Annie Kagan. I read it on another morning while my friend was at work.

There were many parallels between the characters in the book and myself and my brother, Jeremy. Our lives were not as extreme as those in the book—but still, I was a "goody two shoes" and he was a "bad boy." Though Jeremy was not really a bad boy; he was just a boy with a lot of hardships. To me, everything good flowed. To him, hardships flowed more often.

Jeremy died at the age of fifty-eight from lung cancer. That year he had suffered two strokes, got diagnosed with adult-onset diabetes, and then cancer. While in the hospital being treated for cancer, he got Krohn's disease. The doctor said, "I wonder if any more bad luck can happen to this guy."

His life was certainly trying to get his attention. He had worked in Hollywood as an actor—and he played in Hollywood too. He was married three times, the first of which was on a drunken trip across the border into Mexico. He came back with a wife.

Jeremy had cleaned up his act by the end of his life, though. He ran a drug rehabilitation company, and helped hundreds of people to clean up their own lives.

In the book, Billy enjoyed his life, reveled in it and in his hardships. After his death, he flew straight to bliss. He didn't have to recount his life upon death because he had already recounted it while living it. He loved the action and he loved his struggle. His reward was instant bliss.

I have never valued the life circumstances that Billy chose, or the life that Jeremy chose. I would never choose it; it is too hard.

I chose easy and beautiful. I appreciate the contrast, and no longer condemn or judge harshly the choices that my brother made. Extreme hardship and struggle often lead to extreme rewards. Thank you, Billy Fingers. Thank you, Jeremy. I look forward to a world where those choices don't have to be made by anyone.

IMAGE AND ARCHETYPES

"There are several archetypes expressed in the human condition: the prostitute, the saboteur, the victim, and the wounded inner child."

—Kenji Kumara

Sometimes, we use our bodies to prove to ourselves that we have no choice. *If I'm fat, I don't have to... If I'm disabled in a certain way, I don't have a choice.*

The four major archetypes—wounded inner child, prostitute, saboteur, and victim—are at play here. What is your image? What is my image? What is the purpose of creating an image?

The image acts as a shield. It is for protection. But what is it there to protect you from?

We only get overwhelmed when we believe we are in control in the first place. We can't control the infinite. We can only control what is limited—and even then we can't even control that very well.

Commit to following your knowing. Say out loud, " I commit to following my knowing." Say it out loud three times.

You don't have to destroy your old image to transform it into a new image.

THE UNDEFINED

Right is a box. Wrong is a box. Play with the undefined.

If you don't play in another's projection, it knocks them out of their box. Instead, choose every moment to have a relationship with the undefined. We have equated conclusions and boxes with safety. Being in a box does not make you safe.

I think about my reactions to people. Growing up and shutting down. I falsely believed that what they did affected me. What is this energy trying to teach me? I don't need to be fixed. I just choose to listen to the whispers.

Play your part. Enjoy pretending. *Don we now our gay apparel, tra la la la la la la la la!* Value what appears to be a void for the gift that it is.

Exercises for Peace

1. Say out loud three times. I commit to following my knowing.
2. Do seven seconds of breathing. Breathe in for seven seconds and out for seven seconds. Repeat three times. Reside in your heart as you do this.
3. Release your anger. Go outside and yell at a tree. Sit in your car and yell at your windshield.

The **Phoenix** *stands in the calm center, surrounded by fire and chaos.*

CHAPTER 4

Become Peace

"The mind keeps you in the matrix. It can't really solve the problem. The mind can't get you out. Your heart gets you out."

—Rikka Zimmerman

DOUGHNUTS

We were Peace Corps volunteers living on Jabor Jaluit in the Marshall Islands. We had moved from Imroj to Jabor the second year of our service, in 1971.

I held some cooking classes with the local women the first year. It was a long process to cook anything. The village women brought their huge basins and we sat outside on the coral-colored earth in front of my thatched hut. Eggs were available if you went into the jungle areas to gather them. The atoll was so small that nothing was more than ten minutes away. Lime, bananas, and coconut were also available. Sugar, salt, Crisco, and flour were considered staples and came in on a field trip ship, the *Etai Maru*. The ship came every six weeks, which was considered good; some volunteers never saw a ship. Our mail and all our supplies also came on that ship.

I cooked over a wood fire or in a biscuit tin oven. The oven was a small tin with holes in the bottom and coat hanger wires to hold a small, six-by-eight-inch pan. It sat upon a kerosene stove, the kind I had used, at home, when camping. Kerosene also came in on the field trip ship.

I started the cooking class by making coconut cake doughnuts. They were a familiar item—a doughnut—but different, because they were a cake doughnut and had coconut in them.

The class was really more of a demonstration. It took hours to get a pan or to send kids to find eggs, which may or may not have chickens in them. "Wurer yahwey" (Oops! Hello!) was called every time a woman cracked open an egg and a chicken embryo was found inside. You need eggs with whites and yokes, not embryos to make doughnuts.

My yeast doughnuts were too salty and not tough enough for them. When they made their yeast doughnuts, they strung them up on a cord made from a palm frond so that they could fling them over their backs to carry them. Mine were too delicate for that.

Since the cake doughnuts were so different, once we finally got around to making them, they were a hit. As were my cinnamon rolls made with lime instead of cinnamon and my braided breads made with coconut and lime.

On Jabor there was a junior high boarding school. It served the whole Jaluit atoll, not just Jabor. The students ate a lot of rice, but they had no protein and didn't have any money to buy fish. I decided we would start a cooking program to sell lime rolls, braided breads, and doughnuts.

It was a great success, and the students were able to buy fish with the money raised by selling baked goods.

In 1983, a little more than ten years later, we went back to the Marshall Islands in Micronesia. We were in the district center, Majuro, getting supplies in the grocery store. Someone was in the grocery line behind us and said, "Tricia, is that you?" It was one of my students from Jabor.

We chatted about life and I told her we were back in Micronesia and were going to be stationed in Pohnpei. She asked me if I still spoke Marshallese and I rattled off some: "Yahwe yuk. Amun neh ke?"

The cashier said, "Oh, you were in Jaluit. That's where they make that braided bread. They are famous for that." I just looked at her and smiled. Cooking was not my job with the Peace Corps. But it was my passion. Reaching out and sharing our passion in small ways seems to make the biggest difference in the world. This is what the Peace Corps is really about.

I'm still in contact with my old Peace Corps group. My husband and I served as volunteers in the Peace Corps in 1970–71 and as staff during 1983–88. John was program and training officer in Micronesia and country director in Samoa and the Cook Islands. I was chief architect for the Federated States of Micronesia and worked for the United Nations in the Cook Islands.

The Peace Corps advertised their volunteer jobs as "The toughest job you'll ever love." Volunteers often commented that it was "The toughest job you'd ever love to hate." Peace results from the relationships established and the giving of ourselves to and in other cultures. It wasn't really about the TESL that I taught or the agricultural programs that John started. It wasn't about the content of the work we did, but the nature in which we did it. It was about who we were as individuals, and about the everyday encounters and friendships.

CONTROL

Fast forward to 2013 and I am in a power struggle with my ninety-two-year-old mother. I'm providing her assistance so that she may continue to stay in her own home with limited outside services coming in.

> *It is psychic attack anytime you push a thought at someone. Even if you push worry at them. When you think about someone, you get a dump of their universe. Cut the cord and let go of how they found you. Allow the other person to be right and allow yourself to be wrong. Expand as big as the universe and then the other person can't find you. Return choice-making to fluidity. Doubting your own choices is abusive. Control allows you to be controlled by control itself in the matrix. You have made control more important than God. The matrix plays the control battle.*
> —RIKKA ZIMMERMAN

A year later, in 2014, I was still taking care of Mom, and it continued to challenge me. I was there Wednesday through Friday every week for the last three years of her life, and almost every day for her last six months.

For the most part, it was a joy to do so. I drove down to Rockford, Illinois, from my house in Algoma, Wisconsin. It was a four-hour drive, which I enjoyed. It gave me a chance to listen to my spiritual tapes from classes that I had missed or had enjoyed so much that I was listening to them for the tenth time. Four hours later, by the time I got to Mom's house, I was quite mellow and in a very loving mood.

Much of the time, I sat in my chair and she sat on her couch, laughing and giggling about something in the news. She read the paper daily up until the end. I had been known to fall off my chair, laughing so hard at some joke that we shared. We shared what the young people call ROFLOL.

Mom became more frustrated and angry as her mobility decreased and her pain increased. She began to micromanage what I did, when I did it, and how I did it, as I was helping her more and more and she lost more and more control. My frustration and anger increased as I struggled to hold a space of love and peace.

I was in resistance to control. Not allowing was my block. Why couldn't I just allow whatever my mother did to flow through me? I asked myself, *Why can't I see my mother's constant interruptions as something good?* Then I would think, *Peace... flow... react... peace... flow... react.* I would try to allow the reaction, with no resistance. I quit resisting the interruption. I quit resisting my reaction. I quit judging the interruption. I quit judging my reaction to the interruption.

ACCEPTING INTERRUPTION: A THOUGHT LOOP

I would tell myself that Peace comes with the acceptance of all things. Where in my body did I feel the vibrations of peace? Peace went directly to my stomach.

Then I would think, for the thousandth time, *When will her interruptions cease? When will I be able to flow from the peace I have in meditation to a waking, acting being?* I so wanted to listen to an interruption without perceiving it as an interruption. An interruption from what? My state of peace?

I repeated to myself: *Peace, flow, react. Peace, flow, react. Allow the reaction. Don't resist the reaction. Don't judge the interruption. Don't judge the judgment. Peace is the acceptance of all things.* This was a thought loop going around and around in my head.

> *The reality radio station will continue to play.*

Peace is the acceptance of all things. But there must be a step beyond acceptance. What is it? Embrace. Embrace all things— even interruptions. They are here for a perfect reason.

I remember my intent: to be seen and express myself in every moment. To allow myself to react. That would end my resistance. End my frustration.

Let go of how things should be done. Don't distract yourself from what is. Walk through the content. All these energies are born of love. Allow them to return to love. Love holds you in the midst of your tears. The frustration is inside of me—it needs to bubble up. Mother brings it up. God bless her for that. The interruptions are the gift that allows the frustration inside of me to leave. The interruptions are a gift! What then shows up? Peace.

I thought back to when I tried loving my sadness. The sadness got worse...more intense. But that was what was meant by embracing the sadness. Loving it allows more to surface—and it intensifies, but then love dissipates it.

Love is a burning fire. Allow love to hold you in the midst of your tears.

SURRENDER

What you resist persists. Stop working against it and relax into it.

The smile in your heart is your buffer. Carry nature with you wherever you go. That creates the smile in your heart.

The yes runs through my head and out the crown chakra. I hear it as if it was an ancient Chinese saying: *One cannot flow and fix at the same time.*

If you have ideas about yourself, others, and things around you—about how things should be—you react. Your body also reacts to the energies of your ideas.

Melt the charge of your ideas. The electrical charge cannot affect you if you are indifferent to it. Let go of what you don't want. Give up having to control the energy. Trust and allow consciousness to support you in what you want to do.

Breathe, relax, and surrender. Breathe, relax, and surrender.

Is there anywhere to go? Or are you already here, where everything is? Look at the terror. Be bigger and breathe. Look at all of it. You are all of it and more.

I don't have to find what I am supposed to do. I just am.

Why takes you away from your knowing and you get activated by every other fixed position. Reality is a spider web of content—a web of fixed positions. Others throw their positions on us. We need to learn to let them fall to the floor.

Every moment, consciousness is expanding. Fixed positions come up so that we can let them go. The mind is a tool that points to what you believe in. What if what comes up just wants to be harmonized? It's an illusion that you are not embodying consciousness. It's an illusion that you're not embodying Peace. What does peace feel like?

I wonder what the next moment will bring.

THE WAVELENGTH OF PEACE

A few years back, many of the spiritual writers wrote about peace. Deepak Chopra, Wayne Dyer, Eckhart Tolle. It seemed coincidental at the time. Later they all wrote about love. I'm not sure if it was what the world needed to hear at that time or if it was what the world was already hearing. But those spiritual writers were on the same wavelength.

It's funny, the word "wavelength." It is literally a wave of thought. Some people crying out for it and some people embodying it so much that it is reflected to others. The feeling-thought lands out in space. What I used to call the "noosphere." What others call the "matrix," the "quantum," or the "vortex."

We talk about peace on the world level, the country, community, family, relationships, and the self. Peace necessarily starts with the self. One cannot be peaceful with one's co-workers if s/he is not peaceful with her/himself. Peace is similar to and aligned with love but it is not the same. Peace feels more like being at rest. Love feels more active, emanating out. Peace feels more like being focused inward.

But too much definition would lock peace into a limitation.

When I take a deep breath in and let it out, I feel peace on the out-breath, toward the end of the breath and in the gap. It feels like a sigh. After a while, I feel it on the in-breath also. Can you sigh on an in-breath? Yes, but it is just easier on the out-breath. And the total letting go of the out-breath seems to foster more peace. There is an element of letting go of trying to control the peace—that is the feeling I am calling peace.

True Peace is not in polarity with anything else. We think of war and peace. Peace and conflict. Peace and anxiety. While these seem to be opposites, they are not. War and not-war are opposites. Conflict and no-conflict are opposites. Anxiety and calm, or no-anxiety, are opposites. True Peace has no polarity. I guess we could say peace and no-peace. But peace just is; it is a color of love. So no-peace does not exist, just as no-Love does not exist.

CONFLICT

Why does war exist? Why is there confrontation, hatred, fear, anxiety, frustration, and struggle?

Some say that when we came onto this earth, we began to see ourselves as separate from God. We were filled with fear and began to try to control our lives, to control the fear and anxiety that we felt. We blamed ourselves and others for the way we felt—and still do. We control and construct our lives through our intent. We want love but have forgotten that we *are* love. We are born as a gift from God, in love.

But we do not see ourselves as love and instead try to find love outside of ourselves. We are unsuccessful but we are determined. We struggle. Some begin to remember and try to lead the way back to love for the others who continue to struggle.

THE SCHUMANN RESONANCE

The world is moving faster. We demand immediate satisfaction from everything—our food, our computers, our health, and even our relationships. The Schumann Resonance is the rate at which the earth vibrates.

The heartbeat of the earth is 7.83 hz. This has been correlated to the alpha wave of the brain by Herbert Konig. The SR has been called the tuning fork of the brain, and of all natural processes of life. It has also been described as the yin from below and the yang from above. There are places on the earth where there are anomalies to the 7.83, such as the vortexes in Sedona.

Currently the atmosphere is filled with human made radiation noise at different levels. We don't know whether our technology is powered with biocompatible signals or not. Some say that this is the reason that we are growing more polarized.

POLITICS

It is November 17, 2016. A little over a week ago, the US elected Donald Trump to serve as President of the United States.

There was very little joy in the election process. There was much polarity and a whole lot of screaming about what was wrong with the other person, and very little looking forward to what a candidate might accomplish. There was no high road—and certainly no Peace—in that campaign. Most people had to hold their noses to vote. I believe that we can disagree about issues, programs, and process without losing respect for individuals and systems. We should be proud of our politicians and treat them with respect. We should be proud of our military and our police force.

I decided to focus on my respect for the office of president and the system that our country runs under. I also trust that God has a plan and that some good will come from the result of this election. Sometimes we as a people have to bottom out before we can find our way. I grew up in the sixties, when we were not proud of our military, our police, or our politicians. The hippies believed that peace and love were the way. Then they either forgot and or they just grew up. They became wealthy. They changed their views. Careers and families distracted them from what was going on. Maybe I am just an old hippie who still believes in peace and love.

DEMONSTRATING FOR

Protesting should be *for* something, not against something. In fact, since the word "protesting" implies "against something," I believe we should instead use something more positive, like "demonstrating." We should demonstrate *for* peace, not protest *against* war.

It starts with being the peace we are seeking. When we realize that we already are, then we don't have to run around searching for it. When we embody peace ourselves, it's contagious. It's very hard to be in conflict when peace is staring you in the face.

Allow your Peace to spread so that the fear of others dissipates. Then there is less fear around you, and the process becomes even easier.

> *As I change, everything around me will change.*

Can you take pleasure in the idea itself? And allow things to manifest in their own time?

PHOENIX

I first met Phoenix when talking to Nikole Kadel during a healing session by phone in 2016. Nikole is a very powerful earth mother who communes with animals and all of nature. She has a powerful yet gentle presence.

The discussion turned to what animals we had talked to lately. I mentioned Brindl, the bear, one of my spirit companions, and Uva, her spirit whale friend. She had an affinity for both creatures. At that point I said, "Let's see who is here now with us."

Immediately, a bright red phoenix appeared. Bright red and black, with very long tail feathers.

I had never spoken to a phoenix before. I asked him what he would like to share. He showed me chaos and fire. All around me the world was in flames. Buildings, humanity, and the earth all around was in flames. And we could step into the center and be untouched by the fire. Peace is at the center of all chaos.

Peace is at the center of chaos. How interesting. *Stay in our center. Stay in our heart.* That was the lesson of Phoenix.

Frustration, anger, and overwhelm are just feelings. We can't avoid them; repressing them just makes them stick around longer.

So we simply allow them. Or we embrace them and love them into the Peace that happens when they dissipate. We can see feelings in the context of the hierarchy of emotions and then take little steps to move them up the ladder. Or we can be in gratitude for the gift they are showing us: the way back to ourselves, which is spirit in Peace.

> *"Peace can exist as the undercurrent of every emotion."*
>
> —PANACHE DESAI

Exercise for Peace

1. Do the Morning Prayer. Ask God to show you what Peace feels like. Listen and feel.

The **Dove** *lands offering an olive branch.*

CHAPTER 5

Get to Joy

Feel the Sadness, Grief, and Loss

At an architecture conference in 2016 a vendor was speaking to me about logs for a possible architecture project in Northern California. Suddenly he said, "I just have to tell you, you have the most beautiful smile."

That same year at another conference, I walked into an evening social hour. I sat down at a table with a young man and an older one. I began to chat with them.

After a few minutes, the young man said, "Wow! How can I be you? I want to be you. I want your life." I told him to be happy where he was. Soon, he would see an opportunity, and he could choose to take it. But that change starts with being happy where you are now.

Fast forward toward the evening of another conference: I was sitting near the vendors. I had been researching a project I was working on in Maine, a passive, zero-energy house that I was designing for a friend.

I overheard a conversation a little way up the aisle from where I was sitting. It went like this: "You need to meet this woman. She is the most amazing woman. You just have to meet her." The conversation went on. I thought, *Boy, I need to meet this person they are talking about.* And then it occurred to me: They were talking about me! OMG, they were talking about me.

I just walked away, shaking my head. When did I go from being Eeyore to being a woman with a beautiful smile that somebody else wanted to be or to meet?

FEEL THE SADNESS, GRIEF, AND LOSS

We know what sadness feels like. We also know what happiness and joy feel like. Or do we?

I had suffered a great deal of loss in a short period of time. I lost my mom, John's mom, my brother and dad, two horses, three dogs, and three cats. And the rest of my family before that.

I had a lot of suppressed grief. I went about my life thinking that I was happy—after all, I was generally a happy person. But my spark was gone and I didn't even know it.

This book—and in particular this chapter—is how I got my spark back. How I discovered that it was necessary to feel the grief and sadness to get to the other side, which is Joy.

Figure out your sadness! I wrote this to myself in my journal on May 15, 2014. This is how I got started.

> *Our purpose is to enjoy the human experience in all of its facets.*

The ascended body is happy. What is the ascended body? It is a beacon of light that returns people to themselves. Nothing the ascended body says comes from story or reality. The ascended body realizes that all judgments create distance. The ascended body refuses to put itself into a box.

Infinite love doesn't require one to do anything. Nothing is better or worse in oneness. If you try to make people happy, they will try to control you with their sadness. *They* have to choose their happiness. True happiness is unconditional, just like love. You cannot make another person happy. What if one could have total Joy in watching another's sadness? Could you? Yes. You can.

On May 14, 2014, Asia Voight, a local animal communicator, guided me and a small group on a dolphin meditation. I experienced the following:

Bobo the Dolphin jumped and leaped. There were

whale tails also. Talking and walking and spinning.
They were running backward on their tails. I was run-
ning backward on my tail. I was spinning and jumping.
I was laughing. What is the message? *I asked. I heard,*
Have fun. Enjoy life.

Dolphins are the animal expression of this chapter. They express joy and fun.

MOM

It is 2014 and I am feeling sadness, consternation, and a little peace. It has been a time of great loss for me. I am still grieving. After caring for Mom for three years, she died at the age of 93.

These were the words that I read at Mom's funeral, on August 2, 2014. I share these words because I want to show the depth of my love and the grief that I felt at her passing.

Mom,

I am writing this because I know that I will be crying a river of tears. I know that that is okay. It is just clearing my soul from the pain of loss. That is a good thing. I am really okay. I will just cry and express myself through the tears. If I am unable, then someone else can read this for me.

I wanted to share about how Mom was as a person. The obituary gives her life history but doesn't say anything about who she really was. She was an extraordinary person. I was her daughter and her caregiver.

I had the privilege of being her caregiver the last few

years of her life. We were also caregiver to John's mom, Irene. Irene lived with us for four years. John and I planned on living near our parents during the last part of their lives. We were in a position to do it, and we enjoyed that opportunity. Being a caregiver is a blessed gift to all involved. It was not easy and yet it was easy. It was both a struggle and a joy.

As a daughter, Mom taught me by example to love all people. She met people where they were at in their life experience and encouraged them to be even more of who they truly were. She taught me that I could be and do whatever I wanted. She was kind and caring, and loved animals and nature. When we gave her and Mason Katsha, she was so mad. But within two weeks, she learned to love the dog. The dog became the center of her life.

Mother was a giving and generous person. She would give you the shirt off her back. When I was in high school we wore the same clothes. We sewed the clothes together. Me cutting out the fabric on the floor in the kitchen and her sewing at the machine. Then we both wore it. Or we made two very similar outfits. We had fun. Making and creating.

She was always taking people in and helping strangers. She never said no to a cry for help, be it from family or stranger. Her work in mental health was about helping people to live their lives more fully, whether they were patients, doctors, or volunteers.

She was very creative. She was a writer, and a

photographer. She also drew. She loved words, and could out-quip anybody. She was particularly fond of word-playing with Jack and John.

She wrote poems and stories, some of which were in her magazine and others just put in a drawer for someone to find, read, and enjoy. Which I did. Some were cries of tears at night. Others were laughter at the insane happenings of the day. Like when she backed into a soap dispenser with her butt while taking a photograph for a magazine. She tried to dry it at a hand-dryer and ended up with a big target on her behind. She thought it was so funny that she made a Dagwood and Blondie-type cartoon of the event and printed it.

Her creativity extended to her cooking. OMG, the aprons, the hors d' oeuvres, the recipes, cookbooks, and clippings. The five-course meals. Tom and Jerry parties. She would cook two dinners: one to be eaten, and then an entirely different one to be taken home. The second meal was for John or Jerry and fishing camp. She loved food. She even got Mason to eat some vegetables. Although not spinach or beets. She often said that there wasn't a vegetable that she didn't like. Or a person either.

During the last few years, she would sit on the couch, sip her coffee, eat her croissant, and read the newspaper. Starting with the sports page and then she read our horoscopes. I would get on my computer, read something funny, and we would both slap our knees and laugh. I would end up sliding out of the chair onto the floor in hysterics. We had a good time. Then we were off to the hair-dresser, followed by lunch.

Looking good was always important to her. At ninety-three she still dressed to go to rehab and flirted with the gentlemen who were there. And they flirted back. Mom Lesson 100,001: Life remains a playful dance up to the end, if we allow it.

I asked myself what was the final lesson that Mom was teaching me those last few years and months. I thought that perhaps it was about the grace of dying. How to act in grace while suffering through the indignities and pain of growing old.

And while that was true, I realized that it was really about something else. She told me a couple of weeks ago that she woke up every morning with gratitude that she was still alive. She woke up and said: "Oh, boy, what can I do today! I am grateful that God has given me one more day to do something. And I will try to do it as best I can."

I think that was my final lesson from Mom: to live as best I can, with gratitude for the opportunity. I hope that I don't waste it.

Your Loving Daughter
Tricia

That was my good-bye to Mom. Then teariously (seriously) I wrote on March 25, 2015:

> *The more hurt my heart is, the more my mind wants to take over. Isn't that interesting. The more hurt we are, the more our mind wants to protect us.*

I lost my horse Anastacia three weeks before my mom. I replaced her with Polo in March. Polo died five months later, in July.

POLO

Polo was a Midwest Regional Champion Andalusian Gelding. He was in his prime.

I made him a feathered charm to hang from the braid in his mane, using blue jay feathers, and some white and black feathers, as well as white and gold beads. I hung the talisman from his mane and played with him. We danced together.

Four weeks before he died, when I was riding him, he stumbled backing up. He got back up, though, and we finished a very nice ride. He seemed okay but a bit clumsy.

The following week we did a clinic with Ryan Rose. We had a great ride and a very nice private lesson, although the second day we stayed on the ground because he wasn't able to control his hind quarters.

He had a small mass on his hip, a mass on his mandibular joint, and his lymph nodes were swollen. Three vets and the Wisconsin Equine Clinic later, we had a diagnosis of stage four melanoma.

Just keep him comfortable, *they said. I used frankincense and helychrisum*, and raindropped him with oils. I put oils in his water and biscuits. He started giving in to his pain finally, and died the next day.

> *"Feeling is the experience of judgment. Being happy is not the goal. The goal is to let God energy flow through you. There is no digestion of thought forms, just the elimination of them."*
> —RIKKA ZIMMERMAN

I tell this story because Polo gave me such joy, even though he was in such pain. He tried so hard to please and gave so much to me. To assuage my grief, I wrote a letter to Polo in October 2015:

Polo,

I tried to tell you that last week of your life that I was grateful for the joy you had given me even though we had a relatively short time together. As long as you were fighting the cancer in your body, I was willing to fight with you. Toward the end, you no longer let me near you. I understood that on the night of your death you had given up. I saw you give up. But now I realize it was not giving up. It was just surrendering to the great easy. You died in the same spot as my beloved Stacy.

I am sorry that we put you through the treatment at the hospital. I know you would have preferred to just hang out with your buddies and to die there. I was still clinging to the hope that you could be saved.

I was asked today if I would die for you. And would I die for myself. My answer is yes and yes. I know that you died for me. I know now how much pain you were in when I rode you in the Ryan clinic, just two weeks before your death. You gave me such joy when I got on and rode you bareback. I promise to always be that joy.

Your Partner,
Tricia

Then on August 18, 2015, a month after his passing, Polo gave me another gift. What I learned on that day was his final gift to me:

Today, as I drank my morning coffee and allowed the racking convulsions of sadness and tears, I stepped outside of myself to notice that the pain of loss was exquisite. In fact, all feelings were exquisite, sadness, joy, love, hate... all feelings. We are here to feel and isn't it wonderful that we can feel? Life is about feeling. Feeling all of it. Feelings only happen in the "isness" of now. And isn't that exquisite? So even the pain of loss can be exquisite. Thank you, Polo, for the gift of understanding the exquisite pain of loss. I love you.

This experience taught me the value of truly feeling what I feel. It is necessary to feel the pain of loss. To allow it. To go through it. When we come out the other side, we feel joy.

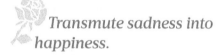 *Transmute sadness into happiness.*

FIVE EXERCISES TO TRANSFORM SADNESS INTO HAPPINESS

These five exercises are something I regularly do. They came from a class that I took with Asia Voight.

Ground every day.

When we are grounded, we are less likely to panic when things happen.

Live in the present moment. Ground yourself. You can even ground your car or your place of business.

One way is to send roots down into the center of the earth. Another is to send your energy down into the earth and then to bring the earth energy up and through you. Another is to just notice that you are already grounded. Noticing has the lightest touch.

John and I were sitting eating lunch. A bohemian waxwing flew up to the window and hovered like a helicopter outside, just looking at us. "Wake up," it said.

Is this grounding in nature? I asked myself. *Is noticing nature grounding in it? Yes. It is.*

Scan your body. Where do you harbor sadness?

Scan your body to find where you are holding on to low or negative energy such as fear, sadness, grief, anger, or frustration.

I am always doing this. First, I notice that I am sad. And then I ask, *Where am I carrying this in my body?* I've noticed that I carry sadness and grief in my second chakra and in my throat. There is also a pain in my high heart.

Where does love emanate from? It seems to go out of my heart and also out from below my solar plexus. Tell that part of your body that you love it and that you will protect it. See the chapter on healing for a complete description of this exercise.

Feel and release emotions.

Feel your emotions. Don't suppress them. Feel, and come out the other side.

I think that I still haven't felt all the grief that is inside of me. In writing about the loss of mother and my horses, I still feel grief and sadness. Writing this book is allowing me to go where I didn't want to go with my grief. Journaling, for some people, is a way to go there.

Going there means going into the feeling and feeling it, until you don't feel it anymore. Then you come out the other side.

It doesn't work to paste happy on top of sad. The sad will just burst through. I know because I did this for a very long time. I was still pasting happy on top of sad when I went to Costa Rica in February of 2015. When I arrived, they called me Eeyore. When I left, I was Cosmic Tigger. How did this happen? By feeling the sadness, until I didn't.

Replace the emotion, remove the block.

Replace the negative (sad) with something else that you notice (joy or love). Early on, for me, this exercise was one of replacing. Now I think of it as joy residing inside, and the sadness is just blocking the joy from coming out. Remove the block and joy bursts forth.

Removing the block means feeling it. Replacing is the noticing of joy or happiness. You are drawn to it by the noticing of it, and being drawn to it draws the joy out of you. Then the flood gates of joy burst open.

Inner imaging. Let go of stories.

Let go of pictures and memories. Let go of stories. Stories hold the negative feeling in place, and feelings hold the stories in place. It is an emotional loop. Attack either part of the loop and the loop is broken.

For a long time I had the image of my mom being wheeled down the corridor to the operating room. This was her last surgery. She was concerned about her hair and her teeth: she didn't want the orderlies to mess up her hair, and she didn't want them to lose her false teeth.

Mother was a tough old broad, and she cared about her appearance even in the last hours of her life. So she gave me her false teeth to hold for her. That was the last verbal interaction I had with her.

Mom lived for almost twenty-four hours after surgery. Then she passed.

After she died, I saw that image over and over in my head. I cried and saw that image. I asked myself, *Why can't I remember something wonderful, like sitting in the chair with her on the couch laughing? Or her chopping vegetables in the kitchen? Why not those images?* I wanted to remember the joy we'd had together. But I just had the final image of her going down the corridor. Or all tubed up after surgery. I carried those two images in my mind for months.

It took several months for me to see different images. It started when I saw a photograph of her, taken when she was twenty. I liked that picture of her and I could easily call it up in my mind.

I now see her laughing on the couch. I rarely see her as old. I see her as the young, vibrant person that I remember from when I was growing up.

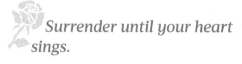 *Surrender until your heart sings.*

I am still crying a river of tears as I write this. The images changed as I was willing to feel the grief. The more grief I felt, the more the images and remembrances I saw. I still feel sadness, but it is a bit more delicious. As days go by I find that I am doing more things that she had asked me to do in her presence, but I had refused. I am no longer resisting her suggestions. I am trying them out and even embracing them as my own.

Resistance of our parents' ideas is a funny thing. It is a natural part of growing up and leaving the nest. But there is also a kind of resistance that happens when we don't want to be like them—so we become the opposite. That opposition is, in itself, a limitation.

I find peace when I adopt an action of mother's. I look up and say, "Thank you for that suggestion"—something that I didn't say enough when I was in resistance to her suggestions, while she was alive.

I say, "Thank you, Mother. I will be you when I use this ceramic defrosting plate."

And I do. And I am. And then I smile at the closeness I feel to her. That is the power of replacing the inner image and letting go of the old story.

ROLLING SADNESS INTO JOY

So how did I get from sadness to joy? This whole book is really about that journey. In addition to the five exercises described above, I discovered that I could physically roll sadness into joy. The following is a description of my experience with that exercise.

I discovered during breath work in Costa Rica that I carried sadness in my sacral chakra. Sometimes when I felt something sad, I felt a burning in my nose, a contraction in my throat, and then a huge contraction in my sacral chakra. It seemed to happen in that order. Over time I noticed the throat and nose less, but the contraction in the sacral chakra was still there.

I asked myself, *What happens if I lift the sadness in the second chakra up to my heart? Or even higher, to my high heart, where happiness resides?*

I did that. The sadness was changed.

What if I raise the sadness to my throat? It giggles.

What if I raise it to my third eye? Joy.

What if I raise it to my crown? Bliss.

Or above that? Beyond bliss. I don't know that realm. That it is the *I don't know realm.*

I could function from the joy realm, but it was too hard to function in the world of reality from the realm of bliss—and it was definitely not easy to function from the "I don't know realm."

So I hung out in the Joy realm. *What would happen if I ran the sadness up through my crown chakra?* I did that. *What if I ran the bliss of my crown down through the sadness?* I did that.

I began to do this every time I felt sadness contract in my second chakra. It became second nature.

Ha! A cosmic joke. Second nature, second chakra.

I felt my stomach contract, and I rolled it up. Rolling sadness into Joy was very physical for quite some time.

Eventually I simplified the process by just running the energy and not doing the physical contraction of rolling. Even simpler was just noticing the energy moving. No contraction, no pushing or pulling, just noticing. Simpler still is just noticing the noticing.

Just notice.

Exercise 1: Transforming Sadness Into Happiness

1. Ground every day.
2. Body scan. Where do you harbor sadness?
3. Emotional release. Feel your feelings until you don't.
4. Replace the emotion. Notice something happy or joyful. Place your attention there—but not until you have done the release. You don't want to paste happy onto sad.
5. Inner imaging. Let go of the negative stories and images.

Exercise 2: Rolling Sadness into Joy

Think of something sad. Feel where the sadness is located in your body.

Is there a contraction or burning somewhere? Contract or lift the sadness up to your heart chakra. Let it drop back down.

Roll it up to your throat. How does it feel there? Let it go back down.

Roll it up to your third eye. How does it feel there? Let it fall back down.

Roll it up to your crown chakra. How does it feel there? Let it go back down.

You can also flow the energy in the other direction.

Notice your crown chakra and then notice your sacral chakra, or wherever you are holding sadness. Then allow the energy from your crown chakra to flow down into the sacral chakra. How does that feel? Repeat the rolling down and up for the power, heart, throat, and third eye chakras.

The **Whale** *goes down into the depths and then breaches.*

CHAPTER 6

Express Joy

I was greeting the morning sunrise on February 15, 2016, in Bimini, and saying my Morning Prayer. At the time there was just peace, love, and joy in my experience of God. The other aspects of God were added later.

The sunrise over the Bimini flats at the marina was spectacular. The pink, lavender, and gold fingered the aqua sea. I was in such gratitude. I was thankful for being alive and for each breath of air. For the retreat I was attending. For the couch I sat on. For the sparkling water and the sunrise.

I asked God to show me how much Joy I could possibly be. How much Joy could God be through me?

I waited and then got showered with a billion sparkles of light. I felt my body explode out into the universe as those sparkles of Joy.

I wondered if I would come back together again or if I would remain a billion pieces of light out in the universe. There was nothing. Just darkness and these exquisite sparkles of light.

I did come back together, but then I wondered if I could walk.

When I got up to leave, I stood up and the ground not only supported me but *it giggled when I walked on it.*

Then I wondered if I could eat and swallow food. I went into the buffet at the hotel, and the food tasted exquisite. Even the water was exquisite. I ran up to people and said that I was so full of Joy that I couldn't contain it. They said, "Don't contain it." So I didn't. I shared it.

And I am still sharing it today. I can relive that experience any time I choose, although it feels different. I can just go to that place of exquisite joy and feel the billion sparkles of light that I am. And this is where the Cheshire cat was born. I became just a smile and nothing else. The Cheshire cat was one step beyond the Cosmic Tigger that I had become in Costa Rica.

LIP SERVICE

It is June 1, 2015, and I ask myself, *What am I giving lip service to? What am I not good enough about?*

I am letting go of the definition of me and my identity. I am letting go of who I think I am and who others think I am.

I am space. Nothing can stick to space. So I expand out. I apply my energy to what I want to be present for. I am giving lip service to being afraid when I know that fear is just energy.

What miracle am I creating right now that I am not letting myself be aware of?

Right now, in typing these words, I realize that this book is the miracle that I am creating. I have sadness for what I am not allowing myself to be, and Joy for what I am allowing myself to be. *Expand out beyond the confines of your identity.* I expand out.

What is there? What is here?

> *Joy is found in the gap between perception and the label we put on it, interpretation.*

PRETEND AND PLAY

It is 2012, and I enlist pretending as a way to engage with the world. Shakespeare said, "The whole world is a stage. We are the players on that stage. Full of sound and fury signifying nothing."

But don't go into the drama. When you go beyond reality it becomes fun. Play, and watch yourself playing; don't believe it.

WATER PLAY

I contacted water and had a dolphin journey (2013).

I began playing with Uther the beluga whale. We played patty-cake with my hands on his fins.

I stood, one foot on one dolphin and one on another, riding across the ocean. I became a dolphin, full of antics. We did backward tail-walking. And then we leaped and splashed.

When we were done, I gave them the gift of krill and shrimp.

I asked myself, What would a dolphin like as a thank you gift? *My answer: the gift of shrimp.*

DOLPHIN MEDITATION (2014)

A woman came riding a dolphin. It was jerky and then became smooth and fast. I saw my horse Temesa reincarnated. She told me her purpose was to help me heal the earth.

I asked, How I am to do this? *I received my answer: more joy and more play.*

The dolphin swished his tail, turned around and looked at me, and then scooted away backward on his tail.

At this time I was still holding on to a definition of healing as healing with my hands on parts of a body. I hadn't realized that Joy and play are my true healing gifts to the world.

ALIGN WITH YOUR VIBRATIONAL ESCROW

On December 3, 2014, I was watching a YouTube video of Ester Hicks talking about joy and letting go of limitations.

We should live in joy with what is. Create by the thoughts that you think. Behavior is not the reason for the results. Line up with choice. Do or don't do. But align with your vibrational escrow.

—Ester Hicks

I hadn't thought of it before, but escrow is something that is out there, accessible when you need it. So I think that works as a metaphor.

I don't have money. Look at my checking account and you'll see. Some people would say that is reality and I can't ignore it. Yes, there is some truth to that.

But you can also see the abundance in what is surrounding you. You can learn to feel abundant. Feel abundant in what you already have and guess what? Your abundance grows. And your checking account grows also.

You do have to take inspired action. Or sometimes the universe takes action for you.

So what does this mean in terms of Joy? How do we argue for our limitations in not feeling joy?

It is easiest for me to think about it in terms of Happy and Sad. They are two polarities, neither of which really exists. But for the moment, let's pretend that they do.

I am happy if I have a car. I am happy if I buy something. I am happy if I have money, love, a relationship, or good food. For me, food is important. I make food important. And I make good food especially important.

But you see, I am doing the making. I create their importance. You can fill in the blank with anything. It is still conditional happiness.

We make our happiness based on conditions. Instead, we could just decide we are happy with the way things are, with what is. Or even that we are happy despite the way things are.

That doesn't mean we can't change the way things are. We can. But we can change them from a place of happiness instead of a place of sadness, anger, or frustration.

You don't have to hate your job to leave it. You can leave the job you love, for an even better job that you love even more. Sometimes we think we have to hate things to leave them, so we create conditions that we can hate, so that we can leave. How miserable is that?

Neither sadness nor happiness really exist. They are just a label we put on a feeling that we experience when the environment presents certain conditions. I lose this. I am sad. I gain this, I am happy. Loss = Sad. Gain = Happy. We become conditioned, habitual, and ultimately limited by these feelings. We begin to choose sadness with the loss, even if we don't really feel it. We cling to it because we think we should feel it. Some people hang on to it as if it were life and death. And for them, it is.

We could just choose instead to be unconditionally happy. When we feel unconditionally happy, it begins to turn into what I would call Joy.

Joy is, to me, a higher order of happiness. It is totally unconditional and seems to come straight from God. Nothing can change it—no comings or goings, no good or bad food, nothing. Joy is everything and nothing at the same time. It just is. And, to me, it sparkles. It sparkles just like the billion sparkles of light that I saw in Bimini. It's pink and gold. It's an aspect of love. It giggles. It laughs. It cries. It dances. It dreams. All at the same time.

I love Joy. I enjoy joy. Truly inspired action is to enjoy.

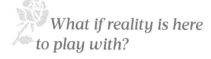

What if reality is here
to play with?

HOMEWORK: What Is Fun?

I was taking a class in 2015, and the homework was to define what I thought fun was. How would I incorporate the idea of fun into my website?

John and I discussed it. What makes up fun? What would a client value? What words could be used to portray fun? What do I mean by "fun"?

I had a job interview for an associate dean position at the college where I taught architecture. The job interview was very peculiar. It was conducted by two people with whom I would be working, but not with the boss.

At some point in the interview, they asked what I valued most in work. I answered that I wanted to have fun.

They were both flabbergasted and horrified. They were obviously not into having fun at work. Needless to say, I did not get the job. Needless to say, I never really wanted that job. It was not a good match for me.

So I had been thinking about trying to sell the idea of fun in the workplace and in the professional environment of architecture. How could I portray fun on my website when most people weren't even aware that it could be part of the design and construction of a building? And what did I mean by fun anyway?

I made a list of all the things that were fun to me: growth, learning, challenge, exploring the world, traveling, quiet, contemplation, sitting on the beach, gardening, walking in the woods, other people's learning and growing. Now, I would add: eating a good meal, having a great conversation, reading a good book, and playing with my horse. But how does one incorporate that sense of fun into the workplace and a website, in a way that would make sense and offer value to a potential client? The answer lies in being all energies, while focusing on fun.

BE ALL ENERGIES: Embrace Even Evil

I realized at this time (March 2015) that though I had intended to welcome all energies, I had not welcomed some. One day during a meditation...

> I saw Darth Vader shooting green lightning bolts at me. I said to myself, "I'll go over here and take in this beautiful pink energy." Then I stopped and said "Wait. But I include all energies."

And then I welcomed in Darth Vader. He was not so scary. In fact, he was quite funny. Then I remembered times when, meditating, I said no to the many energies that popped up because I felt they were evil and spoiling my beautiful meditation time. I stayed focused on the love and the light. I kept them separate and did not welcome in those "evil visions." I did not welcome the evil parts of me in.

I am all energies. I needed to welcome the kill energies, the torture energies, the rape and violent energies that I have judged as bad. I know that I have done all those things at some time in eternity, and that they are a part of me. If we are all one, then we have and will experience all of it. I also know that I do not choose to do those things now. I do not condone violence. But I hope that in accepting it as part of me, it will transform into something like strength. In that transformation, I can find joy.

JOY TO THE WORLD

It is May 2015, and I create space by saying, "Yes."

Yes is the same as space. Density is the same as no. I let new energies come in. I don't label them as fear, etc. I allow them in and get comfortable.

I believe I came here to this planet to show that you don't have to suffer pain and endure accidents to move forward. That sounds a lot like what Jesus came here to do. But for me, obviously, it's more simple.

You can just move forward. You can be aware of but not participate in the stories, or what some people would call drama. Learn what you have to learn and let it go.

I am the energy of fun. I let go of everything that is hard. I eat joy and activate my cellular structure with joy.

I would be true to myself if I was being true to playfulness. What would I choose? What practices could I create every day? I know that I am here to bring Joy to the world. If I had a coaching business I would call it Joy to the World. And the Christmas song would be my jingle.

> *Joy to the world*
> *The Lord is come*
> *Let earth receive her king*
> *Let every heart prepare him room*
> *Let heaven and nature sing*
> *Let heaven and nature sing*
> *Let heaven, let heaven and nature sing.*

What a wonderful sentiment, that every heart should prepare for love. Heaven and nature singing is what happens when we are in love. When in love, we hear all of the birds, trees, and rocks sing. We hear the chorus of angels and trumpets blaring. We allow heaven to sing by noticing that it already is. It sings just at the joy of us. When I smile, all the flowers smile back at me. When I sing to the white choral bells, they ring back at me.

A NEW DREAM

I entered architecture school in 1971. It was my intention at that time to create a construction ship like the *Good Ship Hope* did for health care. Only this one would work in construction for disaster relief in third-world countries.

They told me I was crazy. Of course they also told me I was crazy to enter architecture school because I was a woman. There were only six of us, out of fifty students entering the program. The odds were definitely against us. But we persevered.

I did go back to Micronesia in 1983, and then to Samoa. I did practice some disaster relief in the Cook Islands when they got wiped out by Cyclone Sally. And most recently I took a group of students to Gulf Port, Mississippi, after Hurricane Katrina, to rebuild houses. There is a video on my website that shares the Gulf Port experience.

So I have done some of what I set out to do in the field of architecture. But I wonder now if it is not time to take things a step further, toward that initial dream...or maybe even if there is a new dream. And if it is a new one, I wonder what that dream is... Is it sacred architecture?

"A bird does not sing because it has answers, it sings because it has a song"

- MAYA ANGELOU

Exercises for Getting to Joy

1. Do the Morning Prayer.
   Ask: How much Joy you can possibly be? What does it look and feel like? And then notice it throughout the rest of the day.
2. List all the ways that you have fun. How can you incorporate that into your home life and workplace?

The **Dolphin** *runs backwards on his tail and splashes.*

CHAPTER 7

Reflect Beauty

NARCISSUS

Narcissus was a man who considered himself to be beautiful. He was so enamored with his own beauty that he couldn't stop admiring himself. He would go to a pond every day and gaze into the still water, where he could see his beautiful reflection. Day after day he went and gazed. Then one day he fell in and drowned. Where he had stood at the pond's edge, beautiful yellow flowers grew. They became known as narcissus. That is the story as we generally know it.

But the story does not stop there. One day a man walked up to the pond and asked the pond a question: "Was Narcissus really all that beautiful?"

"What do you mean?" asked the pond.

"Was Narcissus really all that beautiful? I mean, he came here every day and gazed into you. Surely you must have noticed if he was beautiful."

"I don't know," said the pond. "I never noticed, because every time he looked into me, all I could see was my own beauty reflected back."

I had a similar experience in Hawaii, when doing an exercise at a Multidimensional Being Retreat. We each read a declaration of gratitude to a partner and we looked into their eyes as we did it. When I did this, all I could see was my own beauty reflected back in my partner's eyes.

I felt so moved that day that I declared that I would be a Life Transformed Coach. Previously I had said, "No, not me. I can't. I won't." I thought that I wasn't good enough, or talented enough, or that I didn't have the right personality. But that day I thought, *I guess I can. I just have to be me. Others will transform because I am aligned with myself. Nothing else needs to happen.* It was the embodiment of that story that allowed me to move forward. When we see another's beauty, it is the reflection of our own beauty. When we see our own beauty, it is the reflection of the beauty in another person.

How did I get to embodying the reflection of beauty? What is beauty? Are there different kinds of beauty? How does the reflection of beauty brings us home to ourselves?

THE EYES OF THE BEHOLDER

When I think of beauty, I am reminded of the expression, Beauty is in the eyes of the beholder. What I think of as beautiful, the next person may not. Who we call a beauty queen, as in Miss America or Miss Universe, another culture might find ugly. In the Miss Samoa pageant, the qualifications for physique are certainly different.

I would define beauty as something that makes my heart sing. Beauty can also be felt, as in a song, or the touch of velvet. It can be the smell of homemade bread or the smell of lanolin when I rub my horse's back. I salivate when I smell the fresh smell of alfalfa in the spring.

What makes my heart sing? I cry when I see sparkles on the water beneath a beautiful blue sky. Roses in a well-manicured garden. Wild flowers streaming alongside the road when driving. Freshly raked sand in a Japanese rock garden. The Alhambra in Spain. A whale breaching the water. The list goes on and on.... When we see beauty in the world, the world is only reflecting back the beauty that is in our hearts.

ARCHITECTURE ON THE BRAIN

I had recently read *Awakening to the Spirit World* by Sandra Ingerman and Hank Wesselman. It was a book about shamanism. It talked about going in a particular direction while journeying. When journeying you seem to go up or down to get where you are going. The book said that you meet spirit animals when you journey down and spirit people or guides when you journey up, and you meet people when you journey in the middle. Rarely had I stayed in the middle.

The year is 2012 and I seem to have architecture on the brain. I had a dream....

> *I went up to talk to Gabriele and Garland, my guides. I offered Gabriele honey and Garland a rose. I saw a deer with antlers and a lion. Sisyphus was the Deer Master. The lion was Albert, later to be called Arthur. I asked for a message. The deer had architecture swirling around in his antlers. I asked for words. Architecture was swirling around.*
>
> *An old man bent over like Yoda, poked me in the third eye with his cane. A bunch of junk fell out so that I could see better.*

I didn't think too much about the dream other than that it was about architecture. But, driving home from Green Bay later that day, I saw a deer head with antlers in a trash can. Driving home a point. But what was the point? What was I not seeing? I had recently retired from twenty years of teaching architecture. I had opened my architecture business, Silver Creek Designs LLC. I was just finishing The Long House, a small recycled log theater, and was about to embark on the Kewaunee County Nature Center. I was in my head and it was cut off from the rest of me. Like Sisyphus, I was pushing a boulder up a mountain, only to have it fall down again. And I would do it for an eternity...until I learned the lesson. The lesson was about emptying the trash from the mind, and finding balance with the body/mind and spirit.

GIVING GIFTS

A year later, I was reading about giving gifts to spirits before asking for help. I had been doing this, but it was good to be reminded about it. I told myself that I had to address this in the physical world as well as in the spirit world. It is always good to give gifts to spirits and to others. It puts you in a state of gratitude and gratitude is what kick-starts the magic in our lives.

I entered a meditation/journey in which I end up giving roses to myself....

> *I go through a portal on a beach. I see a waterfall. I am sooo hot and burning. I am burning all the impurities out of my body. I stand in the waterfall. I ride the wave of the ocean. I am a pearl in an oyster, a dark gray pearl. I see a person handing out roses in gratitude. I am that person. I spin around and give roses to myself. Giving to others was giving to myself. I was surrounded...and giving myself roses.*

Inspiration is breathing light into a vision.

It is February 2015. I had just started a yearlong coaching program to become a Life Transformed Coach as part of the Adventure in Oneness program with Rikka Zimmerman. The first class was a one-week retreat in Costa Rica. I boarded a shuttle van that transported several of us to the interior of the jungle, where the retreat was held.

On the way in, we saw a rainbow. Many white birds were sitting in a tree. Vines were hanging down everywhere. The site plucked at the strings of my heart, and I began to cry. And so began my journey to Joy. At that moment, Joy was experienced through the beauty of nature.

BREATH WORK IN COSTA RICA:
Transformation to a Butterfly

Walking into the room where the breath work class occurred, I noticed my cheeks felt exhausted—my muscles were stretched from smiling. I had been smiling for at least two days.

I began the thirty minutes of circular breath and then...

> *I dropped down in. I noticed a butterfly on my chin. Then my whole face was tattooed with butterflies.*

My body was wriggling and stretching all over. It was pushing out like a caterpillar inside a cocoon. I was a caterpillar inside a cocoon. I had been encased for so long. It was time to emerge as the glorious butterfly that I was.

I flew and was free. I was fluttering here and there. I was a dark blue butterfly with many colors.

Later, during an energy session with Nicole Kadel,

I became a goddess butterfly with a crown, and a Native American butterfly with a deerskin dress. I fluttered with gossamer wings.

Many of the participants went through transformations at that retreat. Butterflies became a symbol of transformation for me, as they are for many people. They also began to herald or point to something I should pay attention to when they appear. Now when I see butterflies, I pay attention to what is going on around me. It often means something very interesting is about to occur.

GOOD LOOKIN'

When we love something, we can't help but see it as beautiful. Beautiful is an aspect of love. If you buy into a limitation, like ugly, you haven't let go of it in yourself. Love it into the presence of God, and then continue on your beautiful way.

Sometimes things are so ugly they are beautiful. I had a potbellied pig, a rescue pig from Milwaukee. He was found running around Milwaukee and then went home with a couple, who named him Stevie and had him for a few years, until they divorced. Then Stevie came to live with us. I was under the misconception that potbellied pigs were cute. They are not. He came with his toys, blankets, and various paraphernalia. He was very bright. He liked certain people and not others.

One day, Stevie fell in the barn. He broke his leg and we had to set it.

The vet was amazed. He said, "You know, most people would just shoot the pig and eat it." But not us. Stevie's name became Good Lookin', and he was the only pig in Kewaunee County that ever had a cast on its leg. Due to the shape of a pig's leg, it is almost impossible to keep a cast on. We had to duct tape it with a duct tape harness. It lasted for a little while. He had a limp for the rest of his life—which was a long life.

We called him Good Lookin' because he was so homely that only a mother could think he was beautiful. He looked like a warthog. He was snaggle-toothed. Rolls of hairy fat surrounded his snout. Bristles flared down a ridge on his back. He was truly ugly. And in his own way, he was beautiful.

INSPIRATION

There are as many perceptions of beauty in art as there are artists— some of whom strive to make the ugly beautiful, like Good Lookin' was beautiful. When an act of creation comes from the heart, I find it beautiful. When a person is aligned with their heart, I find them beautiful. When music sings in my heart, I find it beautiful. When a building caresses all of my senses and my mind, I find it beautiful. All of nature is a gift from God with love, and I find it beautiful. Even storms are beautiful, powerfully beautiful.

We are inspired by the beautiful.

It is now the summer of 2015 and I am in Hawaii. My friend Leslie Black is leading a small group of us in breath work.

I saw many images after I dropped in:

> There were lots of dolphins and water. One dolphin came up and poked his nose into my third eye. There was a pink submarine-shaped entity that was alive and glowing. You could see into it. You could see all the moving, glowing, energetic parts and inner workings. It came up and gave me a look. It was a living machine creature.
>
> "And what else is there?" I asked. I see Pele, the fire goddess, a presence with a red orange crown extend-

ing across and down the mountain. Fire and burning. I was so hot! I was burning. And then I remembered that fire is also healing and that it can burn through things as it heals/cleanses. The fire is forever in all directions, up, down, out, and sideways. At the same time it is the mountain in Hawaii.

All the energies were of Hawaii. The pink entity became a winged creature. The winged being laid on top of me and enveloped me with her energy. Then I remembered to be grateful. I gave her, and Pele and the mountain, roses as a gift of gratitude. The pink winged creature became an angel, who blew a trumpet through my heart. The trumpet breathed back and forth.

God's exhale became my inhale and my exhale became God's inhale. I no longer controlled my breath. God did. And God breathed me. And then...I breathed myself.

I saw the circular breath as a doughnut breath. The breath is through the middle hole and goes around the doughnut in all directions.

The pink machine had feathered wings. It glowed. It breathed water and the substance of God.

I was arching up in my body. I let the Joy punch the grief and sadness out. There was some humming and the click, click of the dolphins, and the humming was in time with the music playing in the background. I gave a pat to Uther the beluga whale as he swam by. It was a mere hello.

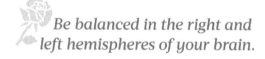 *Be balanced in the right and left hemispheres of your brain.*

SACRED ARCHITECTURE

This spring and summer I created my website for my architecture business, silvercreekdesignsllc.com. I decided that I would focus on sacred architecture, healing centers, and sustainable buildings. I knew what healing centers and sustainable buildings were. But what was sacred architecture?

Sacred architecture is coming home to the body of wholeness.

We build better lives by building better buildings. How does this happen? Why did I choose this profession? I chose architecture because I saw that it offered the integration of the two sides of my brain, the scientific side and the artistic side. Balance within the mind is about balancing the right side of the brain and the left side of the brain. The practice of architecture does this. It is both art and science. It engages both sides of the brain—and the body. Today I would add that architecture also engages the heart. When a building engages the heart/spirit, it becomes sacred.

How is it that a building engages our heart, mind and body? In addition to providing safety and shelter, a good building, at the very least, allows us to experience who we truly are. A great building stops us in our tracks. We look up, out, or over and discover that we stand in the present moment of extraordinary beauty.

We may gasp. And then we breathe in that moment. We breathe out who we were when we came into the space. And we breathe in the present moment of who we currently are, a changed being. When we leave, we take that present-moment experience with us. And we share it with the world.

This is the spiritual facet of architecture building better lives. There are many other facets. Healthy buildings promote health through form, shape, color, material, livability, and function. They also promote health through their use of energy and natural resources. On the scientific side, this could be called sustainability. On the spiritual side, it could be deemed the body of wholeness.

To the body of wholeness I would add mind and spirit. The mind side in science would have us enter into the computer world of smart buildings. These are buildings that light up our life through technology. They start our dinner before we get home. They open the doors for our latchkey kids. There are many ways our buildings can be smart.

So then how do buildings access the spirit? Do we use feng shui, vastu shastra, sacred geometry? We may use many or any of those systems. But what if we simply took a deep breath and came home?

Homes are a place that we come "home" to. What is coming home? Coming home is where beauty enters the equation. The beauty of the space around us mirrors the beauty that we are. When we are in that space, we take a deep breath and we come home to the beauty that is already in us. Our beauty is as individual as we are.

Talk to the space of architecture and ask it what it wants to be.

THE MERKABA: A HEALING CENTER

It is 2016 and I enter a breathing meditation.

> *I was spinning a merkaba* (a divine light vehicle) *like a top. It was going very fast. I visualized a healing center: a double pyramid like a merkaba, with a yin yang pattern on the central floor area. Raised and depressed circular pedestals occur in the right and left halves of the yin and yang, small areas for gathering. This is where feminine and masculine energy are collected.*
>
> *The king's chamber floats one third up and one third down into both pyramids. The main floor is where the gathering of larger groups occurs. The top pyramid floats above grade. Glass encloses the space where the floating occurs. Light pours into the main floor, flooding the gathering area with light. Colored glass caps the top of the pyramid and sends a rainbow of light into the meeting place. Healing occurs both in the upper and lower pyramids, depending on*

whether masculine or feminine energy is needed for the rebalancing of the individual. Masculine energy occurs in the upper pyramid and swirls down in a clockwise direction. Feminine energy resides in the lower pyramid and swirls up in a counter-clockwise direction. Sacred geometries, reflecting pools, and maze gardens lead into the various entrances, which open into the center from the cardinal directions.

God's gift to me is my ability to visualize and design a structure. My gift to God is designing it.

THE OUTHOUSE

I used to tell my architecture students this story every year: how I got my start in architecture.

My husband and I were living as Peace Corps volunteers on Jabor Jaluit, an island on an atoll that was three-quarters of a mile long and one-quarter of a mile wide. It was not very big, and supported 400 people.

When we arrived, there was no outhouse. The local ladies gathered together to squat on the reef at low tide on the ocean side: like a Tupperware party, without the Tupperware.

I wanted an outhouse. John, being the man in the family, decided he was going to build us an outhouse. So he did.

He gathered two-by-fours and plywood and 55-gallon drums and a water seal and even a toilet seat to sit on. And some concrete. He poured a monolithic slab of concrete, sunk two 55-gallon stacked drums into it, placed the water seal into the concrete, and placed the toilet seat on top of the concrete. He then built corrugated metal walls around the slab, and put on a tin roof and a door. He did a beautiful job. It was the most sturdy building on the island.

The only trouble was that when you sat on the seat, it was so far back that your legs stuck straight out. And when your legs stuck out, you couldn't shut the door. If you couldn't shut the door, you had no privacy. So what good is an outhouse with no privacy? It is good shelter from rain....

We laughed because the locals liked to use the outhouse for trysts in the nighttime. The year was 1970 and we had recently seen the movie *2001: A Space Odyssey*. I thought of the concrete as the monolith from *2001*. I decided that from now on this man was not going to do all the designing in this family. I would design our home and all the spaces we lived in—and I did.

I returned home from the Peace Corps, went to architecture school, and became an architect. Truth be told, John is also a beautiful designer. It's just that his particular design for that outhouse did not work out so well. Was it beautiful? Yes. Was it functional? No.

HARMONIOUS SPACE

When I studied architecture, "Form follows function" was one of the first things I learned. It means that the form of a building is "informed" by what it will be used for.

The Romans elevated function into an art form. They developed the arch—which is where the word "architecture" comes from. They built arches in reaction to what they had available in their environment. They had few trees for wood, and they couldn't build post and beam construction. But they did have a lot of stone, and eventually discovered cement.

In contrast, the Greeks developed post and beam construction into a very refined aesthetic, creating the golden mean as a way of judging beauty. The golden mean, or golden ratio, is the basis for what we now call sacred geometry.

When we add the idea of fractals to that, we are copying the fractals of nature. A fractal is the repetition of the whole in each of its parts. Like the leaves of a fern repeating themselves in ever-smaller repetitions. Our mind tells us that it will go on repeating into infinity.

When we incorporate this geometry into our buildings, we find it pleasing and beautiful. The proportion of the geometry and the repetition of the fractal send out wave patterns that harmonize with our human form. We are in harmony and we see beauty. Good architecture combines function and beauty into a harmonious space. When an act of creation comes from the heart, it is beautiful. This chapter told the funny story of how I started my journey as an architect. It described sacred architecture and the beauty of coming home to oneself through the space of architecture. When a person is aligned with their heart, they reflect the beauty that they see everywhere.

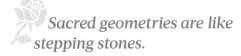 *Sacred geometries are like stepping stones.*

Exercises for Reflecting Beauty

1. Mirror work. Look into a mirror at your left eye. Tell yourself that you are beautiful. Find something that you believe. If you like your hair, tell yourself that you have beautiful hair. Do this for a few minutes every day.

2. Sit in a place of exquisite beauty or listen to music of exquisite beauty. Ask, Why is it so beautiful? And listen to the answer. Know that it is only the reflection of your own exquisite beauty. Then check in about how you feel.

3. Do the Morning Prayer. Ask: "How much Beauty can I possibly be?" Ask God, "What does Beauty look and feel like?" And then notice Beauty throughout the rest of the day. When you see something that is beautiful, how does it make you feel?

"There is something about the outside of a **Horse** *that is good for the inside of a man."*

—Winston S. Churchill

CHAPTER 8

Live in Harmony

"I am the harmony of the God that is."

—Rikka Zimmerman

TINY FISH

In 2015 in Costa Rica our group took a nature walk in silence with Nikole. There was no talking, just silence.

I sat on a rock by the river in the rainforest. A few people floated out on the water, faces pointed up at the sun.

I stared into the rushing white noise of the river. I put my feet in the water and delighted in the tickling wet coolness. Some tiny fish showed up, swimming around my feet.

They sounded like little tinkling bells talking. They said, "We swim together and we let the water take us where it will."

Fish swim in a school in perfect harmony. They trust in the total support of the river.

What does harmony mean? What does living in harmony look like? How do we live in harmony with nature? How do we live in harmony with ourselves and one another?

To live in harmony is to align with yourself. It is letting go of proving, judgment, and exchange, while walking a path that balances feminine and masculine energies. It is entering the now with infinite perception.

HAVING TO PROVE ONESELF

In 2014 I was listening to one of Rikka's monthly calls. She was facilitating a caller who felt the need to prove herself.

I thought about my own need to prove myself. I have always felt a need to prove myself. Mother had to prove herself—and from her I took on the need to prove myself, to her and ultimately to myself.

At this time, I felt that my mission was to return both of us to love, by letting go of a need to prove ourselves. I was doing it for myself, knowing that she could follow if she chose to.

I now thank Mother for everything she did. I know that it must have been very hard for her. Recognizing the pattern is the first big step. Then we can let go of it. *Okay. I am done with this. I am love. Let's play.* It is as simple as that. Simply tell the pattern, "You are done. Proving, you are done." And it is.

In a Webcast, Kenji talked about caretaking our parents. He said: (I paraphrase):

> *You are a pillar holder, the holder of harmony. You are taking care of the parent. You are the counselor. The quantum is timeless infinite possibilities.*
>
> *We are 10 percent mind and 90 percent in the quantum. Don't take disharmony into your body from your parents. You are the counselor, the caretaker.*
>
> *Put ego in the back seat, on the passenger side. You are the navigator. Type in the address of your state, which is peace, love, and calm. Navigate from the quantum. Put the destination of eternal peace in your GPS. It is powered by the field of grace. Save it. Set the destination, and go.*
>
> —KENJI KUMARA

EXCHANGE

Rikka was facilitating a Multidimensional Being retreat in Hawaii in the summer of 2014. I couldn't attend the class because I was taking care of my mom, who was in and out of the hospital. I decided to visit the group through a meditation journey. I joined them in Hawaii on a Sunday....

I saw a man teaching a woman, who was sitting across from another person. They were exchanging cookies like you do at Christmas time. Rikka was explaining that there is no such thing as exchange. The one person grabbed the cookies from the other. Rikka said that it was the person's father that did the grabbing. I tried to remind the woman that the other person was her father. She didn't believe Rikka or me.

A few days later, it came to me that this vision was really about me and my father. I needed to let go of the idea of equal exchange in life. I had seen my father as someone who had taken from me. There were a lot of stories around his behavior. I didn't really know him. Now I could let go of the judgment and be aware of the story.

We believe in exchange. We work and someone pays us to do it. It seems like an exchange; we call it that.

But does exchange really exist? Are we paid what we are worth? What determines our worth? Can we really give or receive? It seems like it when we are talking about cookies.

But when we are talking about something like love, there is no giving or receiving. Love just is. We are love. It spreads to those around us. When we are the other, we call it receiving. But you can't really receive something that you already are. If you are everything, there is nothing to receive. There is also nothing to give. There is no exchange.

EQUALITY

My father had been out of work for quite some time. He seemed to hang out in the basement and drink beer. That was my view of what was happening when I was in high school.

All the money that had been given to me at Christmas and birthdays had been put into a college fund. But when it came time for college, there was no money.

At the time I didn't really notice. I ended up going to college on more or less a full scholarship with a few loans. Later, I judged my father harshly for stealing my money. I thought he probably used it to pay gambling debts or buy beer. I didn't think then that he might have used it to pay the rent. Mom generally paid the bills. She worked to keep a roof over our heads and food on the table. I never wanted for anything. I never felt rich or poor. I really wasn't even aware there was a difference until I went to college.

What I learned during the cookie meditation was to acknowledge the difficulty that my father had in playing the role of weak for me. He played weak so that I could learn strong. And so that I could find and express the balance that was missing in the masculine and feminine roles as they were played in our society. I forged my own balance, neither masculine nor feminine. I projected that balance into my interactions with humanity. I have, in turn, given that gift of harmony by playing that balanced role my whole life.

Are you in balance with your masculine and feminine energies?

I first balanced my masculine and feminine energies by being a woman working in architecture in the early '70s. I didn't choose to try to act masculine. Nor did I choose to try to act feminine. I chose to act as I felt at the time, which was neither. I rejected both aggressive behavior and passive manipulation. I was just me. I had to do a lot of proving myself. I still do. Most contractors still don't want to talk to a woman who is the architect in charge. They don't trust her. I sigh and take a deep breath. I put my ideas forward. And eventually, the contractors come around, with trust and then confidence. Or as we say in the horse world, nose, neck, and maybe the feet.

Most people have to earn trust. People in nontraditional careers have to earn it even more. Male nurses have to prove it in the same way I did. Women are judged harshly when they do the same thing that a man would do. It's not that the actions themselves are *wrong*— it's that they don't ring true to others. That doesn't mean that we have to accept certain roles in society. It isn't about the roles. It's about how we choose to act in those roles. How we behave has to be consistent with who we are.

I recently finished reading a book by Kent Nerburn, *Neither Wolf Nor Dog*. The author had a similar complaint, about white people trying to act like Native Americans and Native Americans trying to act like white people. Neither are consistent with their inherent natures and cultural upbringing. Although much can be learned from the other, each has to act in alignment with who they truly are. We need to be in alignment with ourselves. Only then will our behavior ring true when interacting with others.

It has been my job to act in harmony with my male and female energies. Now it is my job to be in harmony with all else: nature, plants, animals, and even inanimate things, like furniture, mountains, and rocks.

NOW

Accept everything that is going on around you right now. It's all welcome.

We are constantly distracting ourselves from what is going on right now. There is no moving forward. We move forward by connecting to now.

What is required is to act on what you know. Relax, breathe, and receive. Then weave in harmony with ourselves. When you stop, God starts.

Life is a journey, not a destination. When we have clarity and consistency in connecting to our soul, we live soulfully.

CHOOSING A PATH

When I combine spiritual ideas about paths and the story of Orson Scott Card in his book *The Lost Gate*, I get the following idea: Remember the path that you've already walked.

The hero in the book sees the energy of the paths taken by others. He sees them as footsteps of light. He can choose where to follow or choose to take a different path, depending on his intention. He sees the energy of his own path also.

Seeing energy intrigues me. Seeing the footsteps on the ground. What if all choice was just a series of pathways and we could see all the footsteps that had been taken in any direction by all people and ourselves? Would we know any better where to go? Probably not. But it would be fun to play in.

When we are focused on our timing, and not God's timing, we choose limitation. We choose not to choose, and we become the illusionary environment that surrounds us. It is better to choose a path and walk it in God's timing.

I have asked the universe to scatter my path with roses. Then I can see my path, or stop and smell the roses and find my way. It's a metaphor, but it works for me. And my path is always beautiful.

Shamans look for omens to recognize their paths. Ask the universe to show you a way to recognize your path. It should be something that is meaningful to you. Ask the universe, and then pay attention to it when it shows up.

CELEBRATE THE JOURNEY

We are in a constant state of ever-becoming. We will never get there. We say, *If only I had this, I would be happy. If I could achieve this feat, I would be happy. If I had...then the world would open up to me.* That is destination thinking.

In terms of spirituality, we might say, *If only I could see in a certain way, or hear in a certain way, then I would know that I was....* What? Spiritual, a leader, a healer, or enlightened? For me, it was that I wanted to see energy in a certain way. I wanted to hear animals speak using words. Instead I have received a knowing (clairsentience) and a few visions (clairvoyance). Slowly, I learned that this was my way. And that my way was valid and okay.

We sometimes think that we aren't getting anywhere. But we are really circling around, and if we pay attention we might find ourselves a little higher up. We are always evolving and spiraling upward. Let's celebrate the journey.

We should celebrate life. Celebrate every moment and every step, and be in awe of what is around us. Yay! Pick a day and celebrate it.

HARMONY REQUIRES MOVEMENT

Harmony is not stagnant like a pond. It needs to flow like a river. How do we get our energy moving and into harmony? We get it to move by noticing the flow. The following are three exercises that I do to get my energy moving.

TRIANGLE ENERGY FLOW EXERCISE

Run your energy in a triangle. H, imagine the sun at the apex. The right-hand corner holds the body, and the mind is in the left-hand corner. Run the energy around the triangle, from the sun to the body to the mind and back to the sun, to the body, to the mind, and back to the sun. Around and around the triangle it goes. It's a nice way to get the energy moving.

I do it with my hands out and open in a receiving position. The sun is above my head.

CHANNEL ENERGY THROUGH A TUBE EXERCISE

In a breathing meditation, I discovered that I could channel energy through my body like a tube.

See yourself as a tube, with energy running down through the chakras. A series of balls are located in each chakra. Energy flows through the balls, which spin it in both directions, clockwise and counter-clockwise. The energy can flow in any direction, out the front or down to the earth. It swirls around the balls at the center of each chakra. The energy comes down from the crown and out the front of the heart. Or it originates deep inside the heart, goes out the front and back, and then streams out, up through the crown and down out the root chakra.

Each chakra's ball flows the energy around it before it sends it on its way. The energy is rejuvenated by the balls, or the energy is rejuvenating the balls/chakras. Either way, it's rejuvenating!

INFINITY SYMBOL EXERCISE

Picture harmony as an infinity symbol, with past on one side and future on the other. Present is in the middle. Run the energy around the infinity symbol, like a ball running around a figure eight.

Then spin the figure eight like you would spin a quarter. It resembles a donut. Energy moves up through the middle, around the sides, down, and back up the middle. Then spin the torus symbol vertically and in all angles. You have a sphere. All energy leads in and out at the same time. Present remains in the center, but past and future become so intertwined that they are in distinguishable. If you get lost in the visualization, start over with the infinity symbol and then work your way up.

NEGATIVITY

The other morning, I was standing in the upstairs bedroom and looked out the window down at the pasture and asked, "What's wrong with this picture? Something is wrong in the pasture with the horses."

Nothing was wrong. I asked myself, "Why do I always ask what is wrong? Why don't I ask, 'What is right with this picture?'" I let my anxiety push me to worry, then I judge myself for not asking what is right. Instead, I wonder how whatever I am looking at is in perfect alignment with me? Isn't that a better question?

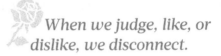 *When we judge, like, or dislike, we disconnect.*

Why do I always start with no? *No, I won't. No, I can't. No. No. And then, Oh. Okay. And finally, Yes. I can and will.*

But why do I start with no? My mother started with no. She would not take anybody else's idea. It had to be her idea. Once she made it her idea, then she would go along with it.

This was a learned pattern. Now that I know where it came from, and that it isn't even mine, I can throw the pattern away and institute a new one. The pattern of yes.

I can start from yes.

When you are around negative people, stay unhooked from their negativity. Let people be where they are without getting hooked into their dramas. Gaze at them with love. Hold the space of love in your heart and know their true divine spirit. Gaze at their spirit when you see them. If you can't gaze into their spirit, then gaze into your own.

When you hold that space, they cannot continue in their old drama. By the grace of God it fades into something else, a higher vibration.

DENSITY

We are living in an age of density. We are getting massive amounts of information and can choose to align with it, or not. Are you aligning with yourself or are you aligning with something else? The universe is constantly asking you if you are ready to align with yourself. Are you ready now? Are you ready now? Are you ready now?

Consciousness will bring everything up for you. You don't have to go looking for it. When you feel an emotional intensity about something, take the charge out of it. It's just one of many positions. If there is a charge in you, then there is something to be resolved there. Resolve it. Let go of the density.

How? Align with yourself and not with others.

INFINITE PERCEPTION

I was sitting, listening to a recording of a livestream by Rikka, channeling the love of God through me. I was imagining myself as a tube of energy, with light flowing out of me, when my computer blew. It often does when a great deal of energy is flowing.

So I had to reboot the recording. She had been talking about how chaos is just God coming into alignment. I was accepting my healing capacity and looking at the depth of that capacity. I was thinking about not caring about the results. God can come through me and I don't have to care about the results. I can just watch the healing capacity of God. If I can just watch and God is doing the work, then it becomes easy. I also don't have to be tied into the result. The result is God's responsibility, not mine.

A woman called in to the livestream and asked, "Do I need to be aware of me being me or am I being me even if I am not aware of it?" Rikka answered that we are always ourselves, even if we are not aware of it. We are always healing ourselves and others, even if we are not aware of it. We only resist the false perception that we have of ourselves. Our true being does not resist our true being. We are so big and so loving. What part of us resists seeing all of that? That false perception is just a grain of sand in the ocean. I swat that perception away as if it were a fly.

And then I have a vision:

I am sitting in a chair. Blue birds swirl around my head and settle down on it and become a crown. I am a king. Masculine. I have broad shoulders and wear royal clothing. I have long golden hair in strings down to my shoulders. I have a scepter in my left hand, with a gem at the top. Light streams down from heaven into the gem, through the scepter and down into the earth.

Then..

I am running around heaven looking through all the lenses. It's like looking out from the Empire State Building through the binoculars—only there are thousands of lenses in all directions. God has all these perceptions. And none of them are right or wrong. They are as big as a mountain and as small as a cell.

"Here in this world we look through one lens. Take me to the place of no perception."
—RIKKA ZIMMERMAN

Harmony is the vibrational alignment of our being. In terms of doing, it is simply surfing the wave of that vibration. Or maybe just lying on the wave and feeling the undulations, in the same way that the Arno School of Love in the Marshall Islands taught women to lie on the waves and undulate with their hips, or so legend says. Being in harmony with yourself and the universe is certainly achieved in the school of love.

Exercises to Live in Harmony

1. Infinite perception. Repeat the following statement out loud three times:

   The more I have no idea of who I am, of what life feels like, of what I feel like, the more joy, magic, safety I am.

2. Pick a day and celebrate it for no reason. Do this once a month.

3. Flow energy down your spine as if you were a huge tube. Send it across each chakra, where you have placed a ball. Swirl the energy around those balls clockwise and counter-clockwise. Start the energy at your heart chakra and send the energy out and around in all directions. Work your way up and down your chakras.

4. Move energy in a triangle. Open your palms and see the sun above your head, and your mind and spirit in your palms. Circulate the energy around the triangle.

5. Move the energy in a figure eight, like the infinity symbol. Visualize the past to the left and the future to the right. The present is in the middle. Run the energy around it. See if you can spin the figure eight horizontally into a Taurus. See if you can spin the Taurus vertically so that it becomes a ball with a center point. All energy leads in and out at the same time. Play with it.

6. Morning Prayer. Ask God to show you what harmony feels like. Show me how much harmony I can be. Then listen and feel. Notice when harmony shows up throughout your day.

*The **Jelly Fish** undulates with rhythm.*

CHAPTER 9

Act in Grace

PRIMORDIAL SOUP

I was playing in the sandbox of God. I stood ankle-deep in God's substance, which I think of as primordial soup. It is usually three-dimensional in all directions, but I was standing in it up to my ankles, like an ocean swirling around my feet.

As I looked out across the expanse, I took my right hand and raised up a mountain out of the depths of the ocean. It was Everest. Then I brought up my hand again and raised a whole range of mountains around Everest.

Then I stood back and brushed my hand over the tops of the mountains. I felt their energy and threw down a host of stars, like bread crumbs to pigeons in the park. It was the Milky Way.

I stood back to admire. Then I lowered them back into the primordial soup. And I brought them up again. Mountains and stars. And then back down into the soup.

What do we mean by grace? What is graciousness? What is the grace of God? How do we enter and reside in the grace of God? Can we embody the grace of God?

I wanted to know what to do or how to be. Then on September 19, 2013 I heard Jesus say to me in a dream, "I have downloaded. Whenever you wake up you will receive it." We manifest by residing in the state of being. The doing in that state is the "non-doing" of being. Ha! This is the gracious act of creation.

When I think of grace, I think of movement. I see a wisp of hair brushing across my face. It is a light touch. It is smooth, like a skater gliding across the ice. It is blowing and billowy, like a sheer white curtain blowing in a gentle breeze. It is always gentle, never harsh.

Irene, my mother-in-law, was always gracious. She was such a gentle, lovely hostess. I often wished that I could be more gracious, like her. I didn't seem to have any graciousness in my body. I was abrupt. I said what was on my mind. There didn't seem to be that kind of softness in me. I was so excited by everything. I couldn't help myself. I had a different kind of energy. I bounced and leapt and bubbled instead of flowing. Part of that was just the energy of youth.

I flow more now. A lot of the bounce has just bubbled off. I love both the bounce of youth and the smoothness of age. The smoothness of aged liquor. Grace with a touch of drunken bliss.

ENERGY MOVES

Energy wants to move. Emotion is energy in motion. It wants to move and not be suppressed.

Your soul wants to live soulfully, *soul...fully.* But your soul is covered over by your emotions, subconscious, conscious mind, and physical body. To shift energy, you must go to the depths of yourself. You must have the willingness to be all of who you are. When we don't experience our fear, it becomes stuck in our bodies. The reality around you changes when you change the vibration inside of yourself.

LOST AND FOUND

What is my focus? I wish to be seen and to discover the expression of my special gifts. It is in the embodiment of total trust that you lose yourself. Once you are lost, then you can be found.

"Consciousness only knows how to harmonize and help you. The hologram exists based on the fixed. Be willing not to exist in the hologram. Be beyond. Then you will know you."

—RIKKA ZIMMERMAN

I allow my body to be space. I am holding space and am an instrument of space. The doorway is an opening. I surrender. It is not a push. It is surrender. I surrender to the grace of God.

BELIEFS AND KNOWING

I keep myself out of experiencing everything. I am afraid. I say no. And then I say yes. With yes, I open to the energetic sense of wonder and gratitude. When we surrender to everything we think of as real, we dissolve the walls. Then we live what we truly know.

My cognitive mind is like a fish out of water. It is flopping around. Allow your mind to take a break. Relax. Tell your mind, *I've got you. It's okay. I love you.* Take your mind with you. I allow my mind to be present with me. *Mind, I won't leave you behind in my knowing.*

Leadership comes from being in alignment with the self. Or aligned with the higher self.

THE SWEETNESS OF LIFE

I crawled onto my horse. Then I leaned over. There was a jar of honey with a small spreader in my hand. "What does it mean?" I asked. "You should spread the word of a sweet life," I heard. Ah, yes, the sweetness of life.

I reacted with denial. *Not me. There's nothing sweet about me. I have nothing to do with sweetness. I am a tough broad, an architect.* Where's the sweetness in that?

What if I am already giving sweetness to the world? What if my sweetness is loving the garbage of the world? What if sweetness dissolves the crap?

When I arrived in Costa Rica, I was filled with sadness and grief at the loss of my mother and my horse. I sat down one evening with an energy worker, Irisha. She listened to my tale of sadness as I dribbled my tears out.

Then she sang a little melody into my ear. It was almost a whisper. The words were just "I love you." The melody was similar to Bach. She sang it over and over for maybe ten minutes.

Something deep inside of me broke. There was such sweetness to that melody. There was such sweetness to Irisha. I heard it over the next few days and even months. I still hear it, and I smile.

Several years ago, an architectural designer friend walked into my kitchen soon after I had remodeled it. She looked at the kitchen and said, "It's sweet. I wasn't expecting sweet." She was probably expecting something sleek and modern. But it was a 1900 remodeled farmhouse.

I had never thought of my kitchen as being sweet. But I guess it is. How nice to cook from a space of sweetness.

SMOOTHNESS

I had played with grace a few times before I included it in my morning prayer. One day I finally included it. I asked "How much grace could I possibly be?" and "What does it look like to see and feel the grace of God?"

What did grace look like reflected back at me? I saw brown silk waving in the breeze. Smooth dark chocolate melting in my mouth. T, likeGrace was a very yummy feeling.

I want to figure skate through life. Skating is just dancing, with speed and smoothness, across a large distance. You move much farther and more quickly across the ice than you do on a dance floor. I want to move smoothly, with ease, through life.

I judged my skating and shut it down. I was an adult competitive figure skater. At the age of forty-seven, I competed at adult nationals. I had some success. One of my gold medals was an interpretive number of me doing Miss Piggy dancing the Tango. It fit my physique and my personality.

Some time later, I quit. I miss it. Perhaps I will return at the age of seventy. I still want to move through life as if gliding across the ice.

ALIGNMENT

I also think about grace as alignment. Going with the flow. Moving down the river with the river and not swimming upstream. Birds catching the up-draft and soaring on the breeze.

I used to play with alignment. I had an alignment button on my computer in my drawing program. I could align a line or object with another one by hitting a button. The alignment command was a very useful tool in drawing and a favorite in Auto CAD.

One day it came to me that I could use the alignment command on myself. I could align with spirit and my own spirit. All I really had to do was notice what direction spirit was going in and hit the align button and then go in that same direction. Things would be much easier and smoother if I could do that.

If you find yourself swimming upstream, try it. Stop. Hit your align button. Then watch as you go with the flow.

SECRET AGENT FOR CHANGE

Rikka called herself a Transformational Change Agent, a secret agent for change.

> When the mind is outside of the heart chamber, it says 'I can't protect you, because I can't find God anywhere.' When the mind moves into the heart chamber, then it feels safe, and knows how to protect us. Receive your life into existence instead of projecting your mind into existence. Putting your heart into your mind does this. When we realize that we chose to be here, we are no longer a victim of our reality. We chose the experience, and we should allow the experience of change. There is infinite possibility.
>
> —RIKKA

When you get ready for the other side of the coin, you create it. What's the worst thing that could happen?

Try bringing your heart into your mind or your mind into your heart. Both work. Do the one that seems easiest to you.

Breathe. Reach up into the highest vibration that you can find. Breathe. Reach your energy down into the center of the earth. Breathe. Do this three times.

Then find your center at your heart. And bring your mind down into your heart. Let your awareness expand out and function in the world from this state. You will find that you will move with and in Grace.

THE UNIFIED FIELD

Movement comes from wind energy. Fire energy can gently melt or sear. Water energy dissolves. Earth energy stabilizes. Energy is completely malleable and changeable. We are embodying something that is totally malleable and changeable. The unified field is everything that really is here.

We have manifested a body. Not only a body—we have dominion. It takes the same amount of energy to manifest a bowl of strawberries, walk through walls, or to bilocate. You are the "Neo" glitch in the matrix of reality. You are a glitch because you invite the world to infinite possibility.

Me and my being show up in everything I do.

SOURCE POINT

In 2015 I wondered what ramifications the use of "you" and "I" had on the center of my being, my source point.

I had the practice of saying, "You are love. You are light. You are infinite. I am love. I am light. I am infinite." For the past year or so I had enjoyed saying "You are love" more than saying "I am love." "You" was more comfortable than "I." The last couple of weeks, when I was swimming or just being, I had practiced equal amounts of "I am" and "You are." I said "I am love" and followed it up with "You are love."

Then I noticed that there was a difference.

I noticed that the "I am" came from a source point in my heart and that the "You are" came from a source point above my head. One was the observer, or my higher self, and the other came from my heart. What came from my heart was more of an embodiment. As I said both equally, the two source points moved closer together. The observer moved closer to my heart.

Today the observer lies low down in my head, at the base of my skull.

MUSTARD SEED

Two days ago, while in meditation, I felt Christ enter my heart. He stood where I stood. I asked myself if I was a tiny seed, like the mustard seed in his heart, or if he was a tiny seed in my heart. I felt if he was so tiny in my heart, that I would not be good enough or have enough of him in me.

But I am reminded of Jesus's story of faith the size of a mustard seed being able to move mountains. And I realize that there is no difference between him being a small seed in me and me being a tiny part of him.

Grace is easy to know, but hard to do. It is also hard to know, but easy to do. It is the ease of raising and lowering a mountain. It is sweetness. It is aligning with spirit. It is the embodiment of the source point of God. It is acting from that point.

There but for the Grace of God, goes I. But...we go there by the Grace of God.

Exercises to Act in Grace

1. Say, "I am love. I am light. I am infinite." Say, "You are love. You are light. You are infinite." Say each three times. Notice the difference. Where does each phrase reside in you? Bring the two locations together into one source point and say the phrases again. You can also use this as a walking meditation. I use it on each step I take or each stroke I swim.

2. Bring your heart into your mind or your mind into your heart. Both work. Do the one that seems easiest to you. Breathe. Reach up into the highest vibration that you can find. Breathe. Reach down into the center of the earth. Breathe. Do this three times. Then find your center at your heart, and bring your mind down into your heart. Let your awareness expand out from this state. You will find that you will move with and in Grace.

3. Create an alignment button. Notice what direction your spirit is going in. Then hit your alignment button.

4. Say the Morning Prayer and ask to be shown what grace feels like. Ask God to show you the grace that surrounds you in life. Notice where it appears in the rest of your day.

*The **Deer** bounds with grace.*
*The **Bear** spreads sweetness.*

CHAPTER 10

Build Communication

Baco! Baco!

We were Peace Corps volunteers serving in the Marshall Islands, living on Imroj Jaluit. The island is part of an atoll. An atoll looks like someone threw a beaded necklace on the water and only the beads stick up. There are a hundred tiny islands in an atoll. In this case six were inhabitable. We lived on one of the biggest, with 250 people.

When we were leaving the district center, Majuro, I meal-planned for a year's worth of food. I had to take enough to last because we didn't know when a field trip ship would come to resupply us. I took enough rice, cans of flour, butter, and vegetables to last. I took a few cans of corned beef, but not many. Most volunteers lived on Dinty Moore beef stew and canned spaghetti. We didn't. I wrote a cooking manual for my fellow volunteers to follow, so that they could eat well utilizing local food. I was a "foodie" and had been raised by a "foodie" mother. I had enough staples to last, but we had no protein. Our protein had to come from what John could catch from the ocean. We had a few chickens. I talk about raising them in the chapter on magic.

We had spent a lot of our Peace Corps allowance on food and fishing gear. Our salary was meant to be in keeping with local wages. We made about $100 a month.

About one month into our service, John had this experience with communication. He fished from his agricultural boat, which he called the "Boom Boom Maru," because of the sound it made. It was a Palauan-made dory-style boat with a diesel engine.

He often fished with three local guys. They were hand-lining for tuna. They would chase an *unoc*, or flock of birds, over a school of bait fish. The tuna would be waiting below to eat the bait fish. They trolled with hand lines that were the size of heavy shoestring. The fish hit and then two or three guys would haul the fish in, hand over hand. The trick was to get the fish in before a shark hit it and all you had left was a head and cleaned skeleton stripped down to the tail—like a cartoon of a fish. Fishing for food to eat is very different than fishing for sport.

John was out fishing with the guys one day when the lines got tangled up in the propellers under the boat. He quickly jumped over the side of the boat and went under it to untangle the mess from the propeller. After all, our livelihood was at stake. You couldn't go to the local store and buy a new fishing line. Every time he would come up for air the guys said, *"Baco! Baco!"*

John looked at them, nodded his head, yes, and then went back down to continue unraveling. He got the line untangled and they continued fishing and brought home some nice tuna.

Two months later, John was sitting around talking to the guys. He could speak the language pretty well. And they said to him, "Boy, you Americans are certainly brave."

"What do you mean?" he asked.

"I mean, you are brave."

"I'm not brave," he said.

"Yes, you are," they said. "You remember when we were out fishing and the lines got tangled under the boat and you went down to untangle them?"

"Yes, I remember," he said.

"Well, you were surrounded by sharks, and you went down anyway. That's very brave."

"I didn't know there were sharks," he said.

"We told you 'Baco Baco' and you went down anyway."

John didn't know what "baco" meant. He didn't know there were sharks surrounding him. He though they were saying "Good job," or "Keep at it" every time he surfaced. So he just shook his head yes and went back down.

What is communication? How do we communicate? Do we communicate face to face, on the phone, or do we use Facebook? Who do we communicate with? Do we communicate with animals, with the spirits, or with God? Can we communicate with a rock? Or can we only communicate with organic beings?

I have described my attempts to communicate with my husband, people, spirits, animals, nature, myself, and God. I say "attempts," because something occurred, but was it what I was attempting to communicate? Was it just noise? Can anything be communication? What forms does communication take?

> *A thought form that is not a question is solidified, a conclusion. Therefore it is a separation. A question is not solidified.*

The senses inform our communication.

While contemplating the morning sunrise and saying my morning prayer, today's word, "communication," came to me. I thought about communication and how it occurs. We input information into and through our senses. Certainly we start with the commonly agreed-upon five senses: touching, hearing, seeing, tasting, and smelling. When I listed them in my mind, "touch" became "feeling."

I thought about verbal and nonverbal communication, part of hearing and seeing. Tasting and smelling are certainly forms of pleasure. Back in caveman days, the sense of smell and taste protected us from poisonous plants. Bitter taste could mean the plant was unsafe. That is a form of communication.

Touch can also be a form of pleasure. We communicate in that way with the universe constantly. How do we communicate and with whom? I have separated my experiences into animal communication, human communication, and communication with the higher self, guides, and the universe.

ANIMAL COMMUNICATION

The following are a series of animal communication attempts and visions, what happened in those attempts, and what I learned in the process of doing them.

THE CAT TEST

Asia Voight, a local animal communicator, put together a test to see if her students could determine the truth of a situation by talking to a cat. It was a practice to build our communication skills with animals.

She asked us if a cat of hers had ever had a litter of kittens. We were to communicate with the cat to find out.

I asked the cat if it had ever had kittens. The cat was very disgruntled, and said "No. Absolutely not." I saw the cat walking down the sidewalk on her hind legs, pushing a baby carriage.

So I answered, "No. The cat did not have kittens." Well, her cat did have kittens. So I was wrong. I thought about it. Duh. The cat was pushing a baby carriage. How could I miss that? I had only listened to the words and the cat's attitude of disgruntlement and I had forgotten about the image. I had been looking for words instead of seeing pictures. And the words were wrong, but the image was right!

When we try to interpret what we see, hear, or know, we often go off course. It is more accurate to just report what we see and not to try to interpret it. Interpretation can cause communication to falter.

BENITO AND THE HORSES

I told Benito, John's Belgian/Andalusian gelding, to stop rubbing his butt on the fence. He had been rubbing his butt for the last five minutes.

I was standing several hundred feet away gardening when I noticed him rubbing his butt. As I spoke to him, he immediately leaped away from the fence, turned around, and looked at me.

Now I often stand in the kitchen window and look out at the horses in the paddock. When I talk to Rhumba, she always looks up and stares at me, even if I know she can't hear what I am saying. If

I talk to Pico, he'll look up from the bunk feeder and stare back at me. He usually turns his whole body to face me when I speak to him.

I don't think they can look through the window into the house and see me standing behind the kitchen counter, 1,500 feet away from them. Is it movement that they see? Or do they just know that I am there?

I don't know how or what they see. But I know that they receive my communication.

JOHN'S BIRD

John has always been a bird watcher. He focuses on the bird and the bird focuses back.

John's bird came to the window three times.

There is a lesson here: be interested and they will be interested in you. The bird was interested back.

THE WATER BOTTLE

In an in-person animal communication class with Asia Voight, we had paired up to practice communicating with one another's pets. We were to try to communicate with them. We had pictures of their pets.

I was communicating with a woman's dog. The woman asked me to tell her what I saw.

> *I saw a dog carrying around a plastic water bottle. It had a blue label. He was just carrying it around in his mouth.*

I told the woman about it and she said that they had controlled the amount of water the dog could have because they were afraid he would pee on the floor. So he wasn't allowed to have unrestricted water.

The dog was clearly thirsty and not happy about it. But she didn't get the point.

At the time, I thought that I couldn't communicate with the dog very well because I didn't hear words. I have since given up on having an idea about *how* the messages should come. I take whatever I see, hear, or just know. Seeing pictures is called clairvoyance. Hearing words is clairaudience. Clairsentience is simply knowing. God decides how, not me.

YODA

A year later, I attempted to talk to my cat Yoda. When assessing my ability to talk with animals on a scale of 1 to 10, I was at that time a 5. I heard at about a 2, and I spoke at about an 8. My seeing was about a 5.

With clairaudience, I find the frequency that I am on, and I match it to the animal. How do I do that? Two ways.

At that time, I created a dial, like on a radio. I turned the dial until I found the right frequency. That is one way.

Now I just open up my heart and allow God.

The first time I talked to Yoda...

> *I saw her as a fox, and a serpent, and then a lion. Yoda was a small gray female cat. She was almost a runt. As I type this she says, "I was not a runt. I was just the perfect small size." "Yes, Yoda," I reply.*

It is very hard to write about a past communication with an animal without them piping in at the current moment, as I write...

> *She pawed my face. The serpent ate at my third eye. We were heart to heart.*
>
> *I told myself:* Allow. Don't push. Focus with hands on your heart. Brain off and feel.

I forgot to ask her for permission to speak to her. But I did remember to thank her.

Anyway, Yoda was funny, because her name was Yoda and her message to me was about power and size. We named her Yoda because of the expression on her face, when her ears were out to the side. Her face looked just like Yoda.

*Visions are the containers
for divine wisdom, same as
words, or brushstrokes.*

TEMESA: The Sea Healer

I was in tears because my horse Temesa had died earlier that summer. She was very old and had a good life. Her organs were shutting down, and we tried to ease her pain and were willing to help her if she wanted to fight for her life.

She was very angry and frustrated by her inability to eat and drink. She fought to do so. We had the vet over three times. And so we fought for her also.

Her passing was painful for her. She fought up until the end, when her heart finally gave out. *Boom.* She went down. And that was that.

She was a beautiful Andalusian mare, who gave us Pico. She was full of anxiety and spitfire. I miss her. But I know that she is at peace and out of pain.

> *A woman was riding on a dolphin. It was jerky, then it was very smooth and fast. It was my horse Temesa. Perhaps this was the sea healer. She was reincarnated to heal the earth. My hands hold parts of bodies and heal with energy. A stick pokes my second eye. I ask, "How am I to do this?" I feel that I need to see energy in middle earth. My answer is "more joy and play." To think of her as Temesa the sea healer makes me smile. It eases the pain in my heart.*

TRUST AND FOCUS

What I needed at that time was a poke in the eye. A bird flew into the window, taking me away from the negative stuff I had been thinking about.

In the early stages of animal communication, we look for easy yes and no answers. My horse shaking her head was yes. Up and down or side to side as a human would do. To head shaking I added pawing, for clearer confirmation of a no.

My visions took off as I learned to trust the pictures and my know-ing, instead of always asking for yes and no answers. Then the head shaking and pawing became unnecessary.

I get inklings. I tell myself to expand into the inkling, be well-grounded. We can use shapes, triangles, circles, sacred geometries. These can focus our attention.

Morphing or shapeshifting is another kind of practice. It can focus our attention. Morphing is when you turn into the animal. You become it. Shamans sometimes become animals. Shamans like Juan Matus, as described in *Tales of Power* by Carlos Castaneda, can become a crow.

Sometimes things are very distant. When they are far away, it seems to take a great deal of energy to get there. If we are well-grounded, then things move closer to us. Grounding makes it easier. I used to think I had to be close to an animal to communicate with it. I let time and space stop me from communicating. I later learned that time and space were not a deterrent to communication. Some-thing could be dead or on the other side of the planet, and it made little difference to communication. Now I know that all you have to do is open up your heart and allow. Energy pours in with the open-ing. I ground and allow.

THE ANIMALS

The animals seem to represent each chapter of this book. Accord-ingly, each chapter is anchored by an animal sharing his wisdom.

The **spider** spins his web. You become stuck in fear.
Chapter 1. You access love by going through fear.

The **dog** is about unconditional love, companionship, and service. Chapter 2. You allow love.

The **phoenix** transforms chaos into peace. Chapter 3. The phoenix shows the way through the chaos of anger and frustration to the calm of peace.

The **dove** offers an olive branch in peace. Chapter 4. You become peace.

The **whale** breaches from the depths. Chapter 5. You get to joy by feeling the sadness, grief and loss.

The **dolphin, bluebird** and **duck** all represent chapter 6. They express joy directly. The **dolphin** is about fun and joy. They love to cavort and are always smiling. They run backward on their tails and spin into the air. Why? Because they can! The **duck** is about happiness. They quack away and laugh at my jokes as I laugh at theirs. And of course there is the **bluebird** of happiness, which sits on my left shoulder and chirps away at me, *Be happy!*

The **horse** is about freedom, beauty, and the present moment. Chapter 7. He expresses the reflection of beauty. The beauty of my horse always makes me smile.

The **jellyfish** undulates with rhythm. Chapter 8. He lives in harmony with his surroundings.

Both the **deer** and **bear** represent Chapter 9. We act in grace with power, sweetness, and movement. The deer bounds with Grace.

The **ants** are always in communication with one another and the hive. Chapter 10. From them we can learn to build communication.

Bees gift us their honey. Chapter 11. Their honey heals with love.

The **pig** wallows in abundance. Chapter 12. He stores our abundance in his fat little body bank.

The **butterfly** is about transformation with ease, allowance, and lightness. He emerges from the primordial soup of his cocoon. Chapter 13. He flutters by and I am grateful.

Both the **dragon** and the **unicorn** represent chapter 14. The dragon is about transformation and power. He is magic and goes into all places, in all times. He breathes fire. The unicorn also appears in magic. He flies.

The **lightning bug** shines his light outward in quick

bursts. He represents Chapter 15. He demonstrates the explosion into bliss.

The **snake** winds and unwinds. The truth is hidden and then it strikes. He represents Chapter 16. He speaks the truth.

The **giraffe** reaches down with his long neck. He represents Chapter 17. His legs and neck are in divine perfection.

Man and woman represent Chapter 18. Together as human animals they co-create in harmony.

 *Write from being.*

HUMAN COMMUNICATION

The following sections are about the discoveries I had in communication with people. The act of writing this book caused me to think about many of them.

Writing

Ultimately, the writing has to come from and through me. It is false when I try to wear another person's cloak of words. The "literarians" say that writers have to find their own voice.

I agree. I would describe my voice as a truth that comes through me.

I can only write from my own being. How do I do this? Well, it starts with words.

Words

I like to make up my own words. Like "literarian." Sometimes two words aren't quite right on their own, but if I combine them into a new word they are just right—even if the word didn't previously exist. English grammarians will hate me. I don't care. It's fun.

A good example is the word "flutterby," a combination of "butterfly" and "flutter." It is much more descriptive and, I think, accurate to call it a "flutterby." So I do. This is me writing from my being.

Words are symbols. They represent a thing but they are not that thing. A table is a thing. But the word "table" is not a table. And when we say a word to another person, they may or may not get the same picture of the word in their mind that we have in ours. Words can limit the things we describe. There are not enough words in the English language to totally describe a thing. But they are the best tool we have to communicate with until we can use direct telepathic communication—at which point there will be nothing to communicate, because we will all know all things. Until that time, we have agreements about the meanings of words.

Don Miguel Ruiz in *The Four Agreements* says that we should be impeccable with our words:

> *"Being impeccable with your word is the correct use of your energy; it means to use your energy in the direction of truth and love for yourself. If you make an agreement with yourself to be impeccable with your word, just with that intention, the truth will manifest through you and clean all the emotional poison that exists within you."*

Okay. So I am impeccable with my word and I speak from my truth. But there is still a problem. I say to my husband, "What a beautiful blue sky today."

And he says, "What shade of blue? I mean, there are at least fifty shades. Is it azure or aquamarine or what?"

I say, "It's blue!"

Linear v. Global

John thinks linearly, in a straight line. He says that I am a cricket that jumps here, there, and everywhere in time and space. He is specific and linear. I am general and holistic. He gets frustrated with my jumping from one thing to another, because he can't follow it with his linear thinking process. I get frustrated with how long it takes him to get to someplace, because he has to follow his thought along a certain path. I get bored staying on that path. So communication between us can be a challenge.

With respect, love, persistence, and allowance, communication happens. From my perspective, we don't have to do or say anything. Communication is already happening through our hearts. It's just our minds that get in the way. Holistic thinking occurs on the right side of the brain, and linear thinking on the left side. When we have lots of synapses that cross the two sides, we are able to do both. Architects have to create from both sides of their brain; the degree to which they are able to do this is reflected in the kind of buildings that they are able to design.

John uses lots of complicated words to describe a situation. He believes it makes him more accurate. I believe that the general is more accurate, because it is less limiting and separates less from the truth of what is.

Nerburn, in *Neither Wolf Nor Dog*, talks about how the white man can't appreciate silence. He says that the white man can't stop talking and uses too many words when he does. The traditional Native American, he says, only spoke when he had something important to say.

I appreciate silence, impeccable words, simplicity, and just enough detail to impart clarity of ideas. Oh, and I like to have a bit of fun.

ORIGINS OF HAWAIIAN LANGUAGE

In a meditation, I spoke to some dolphins. The dolphins spoke back.

> *I asked him his name. He said,* Eee...click....aaaaah. Eeee, in-breath. Click... glottal stop. Out-breath, aaaaah. *I realized that in addition to his name, this was the origin of Hawaiian language. Their language came from the language of dolphins.*

When I hear the Hawaiian language spoken, I can hear the dolphins speaking through it.

COMMUNICATION WITH SELF AND THE UNIVERSE

Thinking about communication led me to consider knowing and belief. I would normally put the difference between knowing and belief in the category of truth. Knowing is a communication of truth from the universe. Belief is a construct of the mind based on past experiences. It is a communication of the mind: from the mind and to the mind.

Belief might become knowing if the content falls into the category of the truth. But if it is just a belief, we might make it a reality, but it is not the truth. By reality I mean the experience we have as we make our way on this earth.

Wisdom is acting on the knowing of truth. Acting on a belief might be "fake it until you make it" and it might become a knowing. If it is just a belief, then you could create "stickiness" or even misery in your life through the power of your limiting belief. Noticing the feelings and what shamans call signs that the universe sends us is indeed communication with the universe. We are in communication with the universe when we notice our feelings and when we notice signs.

FORMS OF COMMUNICATION

With people, when we want to communicate, we usually talk. Some of us also gesture—and some, like my husband, gesture a great deal.

His mouth is hard-wired to his hands. In fact, I have tied his hands, to see if he could talk with no hands. He can't.

In communicating with people, we see and interpret based on our belief systems. With animals, we talk and also gesture. Sometimes, as with horses, we only gesture or communicate through body language.

Some of us also communicate with our chi energy. And sometimes our chi is added whether or not we are aware of it.

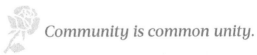 *Community is common unity.*

INTUITION

There is also what we feel and know in the presence of others. If we are wise, we let go of our beliefs and act on our knowing, which is centered in our heart and sometimes called intuition. It might also be located in our gut.

With practice, we can become quite adept at listening to our heart/ gut. The mind is there to keep us safe. Sitting in our hearts, we are always safe.

To quiet my mind, I give it something to do. Go figure this out. Go over there and play with these ideas. My mind is very active and I always have to give it something to do. It likes to explain.

That's nice, I tell it. *Great ideas.* Then I tell it, *Now let's ask the heart what it knows.* Then I listen to my heart. My mind can then rush off to a new explanation.

My mind is not bad or wrong. But it likes to take credit for what my heart comes up with. So I let it.

The ego isn't necessarily bad or wrong either. It just needs to follow the heart. The heart is the well source. The mind gives the well source beautiful definition and detail: it puts icing on the cake and all sorts of decorations. The mind can offer rich, intricate experiences.

What is the feeling tone of intention? The essence of the vibration of your soul song.

EDITING OURSELVES

In 2015 I asked myself, what part of me is sabotaging me? What stuff do I need to rewrite in order to transform? What do I need to rewrite so that other people can transform? I go deep into my heart and ask, *What is the next step?*

> *Not to be afraid of superpowers coming in. So tapped in, so turned on. Overwhelmed? If you have the presence of Jesus, How would you feel? Are you ready to move out of conflict? In spite of their lying, I am going to see them in their highest light/soul. When egos try to communicate, they want to have their own way. Call for help in healing. We hold space for those. It's your presence. Holding space is too much like doing. Presence without doing.... Move our attention into the realm of light. Let's receive an anti how wave. Manner of approach? How we approach life.*
>
> —Kenji Kumara

COMMUNICATING WITH GUIDES

I visited a friend in San Francisco. We went to her vacation home in the redwood forest. She was just starting to channel an entity named Elias. We began by breathing, sitting in two comfortable chairs. This is what Steff/Elias told me.

> *I would meet Maru, an Indian, who would help me on my journey with horses. I was wondering why I wanted to paint a blue circle around Polo's left eye and braid blue feathers with beads into his mane with a single braid. There is nothing Native American about Polo or me. Yet for the past two months I had wanted to do this. I had gathered one black feather before I had come to California. My gift of expression seems to be in my being. Mother is happy and we were best friends.*

Then Steff gave me several blue feathers from a blue jay. I had thought to gather some when I saw the bird. Then I discovered that she had already gathered many. And she gave some to me.

When I look back on this experience, I am reminded that I had a guide long ago, whom I called Elliot. He seemed similar to Elias. Also, I had been given the name of Maru for myself in a past-life journey that I had done a couple years earlier. The time was 1876, and I/he hunted buffalo. I was a warrior and had a black eagle-feather breastplate. Now my previous self is going to help my current self. Sometimes I call on Maru to help me with the horses. I say *Maru, how should I deal with this?* And sometimes an answer comes. *Nay.* Or should I say *Neigh.* An answer always comes—it's just that sometimes I remember to listen.

It is a yes for them because it is a yes for you.

SHAMANIC JOURNEY

In Hawaii, I led Leslie and Cheryl (not her real name) on a shamanic journey. We were sitting on the Big Island in Kona, breathing in the sunset over the water. We basked in the glow of the light. I led them on a journey to talk with dolphins, to prepare us for our dolphin swim the next day.

We took a walk on the beach. Found a secluded spot and sat down. We watched the waves. We walked out into the distant water. I invited whoever was there to come in to journey with us.

Pe Eoki, a turtle, showed up for Leslie. She spent time with him and rode on his back. He told her that her belly was not just a source of power in giving, but it was also about receiving.

Leslie had major belly issues and a hernia. On the day before, she had swum with a turtle, who rubbed against her belly. And then she stood on him, in the water. That evening I bought her a painting of a tribal turtle by a local Hawaiian artist. The turtle was in her colors of green and orange.

A dorado fish showed up for Cheryl. His name was Sarud. Cheryl was from Trinidad and was in search of a healer to heal her knee. Sarud had a private conversation with Cheryl. I gave her a painting of a tribal dorado that looked like Sarud.

COSMIC COINCIDENCES AND CONNECTIONS

John

I was staying at the Moana Lana hotel in Hawaii with Leslie. We were attending a multidimensional being retreat. I got up at 5 a.m. to do my Morning Prayer before the sessions began. Leslie was still asleep.

I made coffee to take with me to the beach. The coffee overflowed and spilled down the front of the cupboard. I cleaned up the mess, got my coffee, and proceeded to go outside to embrace the sunrise.

John called. He was drinking his morning coffee. He was upset because his coffee had overflowed and had spilled down the front of the cabinet. I told him what had happened to me. He was in Wisconsin. I was in Hawaii. He said, "Talk about cosmic coincidence and connection."

I just laughed. John and I have been married for fifty-plus years. We have a lot of connections.

> *A cosmic coincidence is a conversation that you are having with the universe.*

Virginia

I had another cosmic coincidence when I was on a long drive listening to a recording of a class that I had missed. . I suddenly thought about Virginia, a woman I had met in Bimini. I had been talking about designing a healing center for her. I thought about the pyramid she wanted for her center and thought, *I should give her a call and start work on her project.*

Suddenly, over the car stereo, up pops Virginia from the retreat, asking a question, I'm thinking of her and she shows up to ask a question.Our lives are punctuated with cosmic coincidences. We just need to pay attention to them. The more we pay attention to them, the more they show up. The more they show up, the more we pay attention. Until…I guess until we are in complete co-creation with the universe.

> *The universe doesn't hear words, just the vibration of the intention of the words.*

The universe is always in communication with itself. Sometimes, we participate in that communication. It can be with nature and animals. It can be in the form of talking, knowing, or just noticing that there is always something deeper happening, which we could be aware of if only we chose to.

Noticing means that the universe has successfully communicated with us. It notices us, and we notice it.

As Dan Millman says in *The Way of the Peaceful Warrior*, "There is never not something happening." There is always something happening. We just need to notice it. That is communication.

 *Energy echoes.*

Exercises to Improve Communication

1. For grounding: Feel into the earth with the energy of your feet. Tickle the center of the earth. Take a deep breath. Do this three times.

2. For knowing: Go into your heart. Expand out as big as the universe. Ask your heart what it knows about this. Ask all of your questions from this place. Communicate from this place of knowing.

3. To communicate with animals: Open your heart and listen. Ask permission, listen, and give thanks. If you can't quite hear, turn the dial on the radio of your heart until you have the right frequency. It takes practice.

4. For opening: Say the Morning Prayer and ask to be shown what communication looks, feels, and sounds like. Ask God to show you the communication that occurs in your life. Notice how it appears in the rest of your day.

The **Ants** *are constant communication at work.*

CHAPTER 11

Heal with Love

I was driving down the highway to my mom's house, a four-hour drive. About an hour and a half in, I got a huge pain in my right shoulder.

I'd had it before a few times. It was excruciating. I thought I was going to have a heart attack and die. I thought maybe I should pull over. But then I thought, No. I will ask this pain why it is here and give it love.

"Why are you here?" I asked. I heard, "Love."

I thought, *I am love. Love is all there is. I love you.*

But it was very hard to love the pain. It hurt! I couldn't actually love the pain, but I was grateful to the pain for showing me that I was not currently being all the love that I could be. I could love that.

I breathed through the pain and tried to relax. I kept repeating "I am love. You are love. I love you" to the pain. A few miles down the road, I noticed that the pain was gone.

I was amazed. It was really quite easy. I loved the pain and it left.

> *Heal ourselves and we heal others. Heal others and we heal ourselves. Because we are one.*

You can't resist pain and love it at the same time. When you resist, you contract and hold the pain in place. You can't love it with the intention that it will go away. That would mean that you don't really love it.

You can only love it because you actually do love it. How do you do this? You can love the message. You can love who you are, which is love. You can love the act of love. I love me loving me.

The shoulder pain has shown up a couple of times since then, but only mildly, more of a nudge then a slam in the face. What if we listened to tickles and whispers as much as we did to in-your-face pain? Allowing it to be a whisper or a tickle, which is much better than pain. For that to be our norm, we have to notice, listen to, and act on the whispers.

> *"Pain is an experience meant to be released. Experience it from God presence. Be in it with God love. That transforms the experience. Pain is not wrong. It is just an experience."*
> —RIKKA ZIMMERMAN

What is healing? Can we heal ourselves? How do we heal ourselves or others? How does healing happen? I have grouped the answers to these questions into two categories: the body, and the mind/spirit.

We live our lives validating limitation, which traps pain and illness in the body. To live with love in your heart is to free the body and mind from limitation.

In my journey, the sequence of events was: I discovered my own process; I discovered my own well-being; I became a "healer."

MY JOURNEY AS A "HEALER"

My journey toward becoming a healer has been a long and convoluted one. For many years I read every book about healing I could get my hands on. I read hundreds of books. I read all of Deepak Chopra's books, Carlos Castaneda, Eckhart Toll, Wayne Dyer, Shirley McClain, and many others. I read about herbs, Chinese medicine, Ayurveda, the Toltec ways, and Shamanism. I was influenced by natural medicines, psychic surgery, acupuncture, the healing power of touch, and reiki.

Somewhere in all of that knowledge, I developed an idea about what I thought a healer is/does. I thought that psychic surgery was really cool. I told myself, *I'd like to do that.*

I also knew that healing was tied to our belief construct. It's called the Pygmalion effect. If you believe someone or something can heal you, it can. If you believe it will, it will. I had no one to talk to about any of this, though, and I thought I was perhaps just a little crazy. But I continued my avid reading and meditations.

At some point, I decided that I should be a healer. I was already an architect, so I didn't need another profession per se, just an avocation. I loved architecture. So I thought I would heal people part-time.

At this point in my life, I didn't have many friends and I stayed away from people for the most part. I was shy. People judged me as aloof.

Around this time, I studied with an animal communicator, Asia Voight. I thought talking to animals was great. It occurred to me that I should heal animals instead of people.

I rationalized that people ought to just heal themselves, and that anything I could do to assist them would just be temporary, because the real healing would have to come from themselves anyway. I had a lot of judgment at that time, and judged people as wrong because they didn't heal themselves. I shared my misgivings on healing people with a woman in my animal communication class. She was horrified and judged me as uncaring. I kept my ideas about healing to myself after that.

Animals deserved my healing. They didn't deserve to be sick.

I played with animal healing for a while, until I realized that animals didn't need my healing either. They could heal themselves just fine. I could assist them, but they really didn't need my help.

So then I thought how about the earth. I could heal the earth. Now I realize that the earth doesn't need my healing either. I had taught green architecture and the healing of the planet for twenty years. I currently believe we should act on behalf of the earth, but from a place of Joy and abundance, not from a place of despair and lack.

Then I asked myself, Now what? I didn't recognize at that time that I could be a catalyst for others to heal themselves from within. Now I understand that in my presence people can heal themselves, when I carry enough energy and abide in love. That process is what we call healing.

I now also know that people did nothing to deserve their pain and suffering. And further, ailments are just the bread crumbs that remind us of our way as we travel home to ourselves. To "heal" others is to rob them of that journey.

I seem to have come full circle.

WE ARE ALL HEALERS

At about that time, I heard Rikka Zimmerman say, in a webcast, that we are all healers, even if we are doing plumbing. It just so happened that at that exact moment I was working on the plumbing for an architecture project that I was designing. I had to let go of my definitions of healing. I could do plumbing and still do healing.

Shortly thereafter, I came up with the idea of sacred architecture. My *buildings* could be healing.

I now realize that this is still a definition and all definitions limit us. We are all healers, no matter what we are doing.

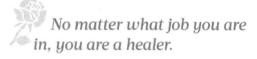 *No matter what job you are in, you are a healer.*

CHANGE AS HEALING

When we share ourselves with another, a synchronicity happens. We should share ourselves, rather than gossip about the other person or judge them.

To create change in ourselves, we must be the change we want to see.

To create change in another, we must be ourselves and share it with the other. Then the other changes. S/he does not change because we want her/him to. Change happens through acceptance, allowance, and embracing what is. This change is, in itself, healing.

VALIDATING A LIMITED WORLD

If you have density in your body, make it not matter. Don't be conclusionary. Don't stack conclusions on top of it. The more joy you have with it, the easier it is to change. Make it sunny and more joyful. Heavy, dense energy locks it into your system. We analyze our body. That puts energy on reality and our body staying the same. Instead, say, 'Oh, this is what is showing up. And what energy can I add to this to let it go?' Let go of all the density paradigm. If you feel bad for others, you are actually validating the limited world they live in.

—RIKKA ZIMMERMAN

Fast forward to 2016. I had an experience of "validating a limited world."

I went to visit an old friend, named Margaret (not her real name), in a nursing home. She had fallen and her friend, Alice, had put her in the institution.

Margaret was full of hatred and anger. She kept repeating that her friend had told lies about her. She didn't need to be there. Yes, she had fallen, but she was okay. She was worried about her house. She thought Alice had put her in the institution so that she could steal her house, or at least steal all of the things in it.

Margaret and I had enjoyed lunch together once a month for the past sixteen years. The previous couple of years, though, it had been more sporadic. She stood me up a couple of times.

The last time, she had called me the night before and asked, "Are we having lunch tomorrow?" I said yes. And then she was a no-show.

She wasn't answering her phone, which wasn't unusual. Having a cell phone was a new thing for her. She didn't answer her door either, because she didn't want anyone to see her house. I suspected that she was what some people might call a hoarder.

Later, Bill told me that she was in the nursing home. Bill had taken care of her house for years.

Margaret had feared this very situation. Her best friend had been put into an institution against her will, and Margaret was afraid that the same thing would happen to her. She refused to let Meals on Wheels into her home and wouldn't answer her door—so the county declared her incompetent and put her in permanent care in a nursing home.

While hateful and angry, she still managed to enjoy some of it, playing cards and making crafts. But she wasn't going to let go of the idea of returning home. Although she feared that soon there would be no home to return to.

I continued to visit her, in the nursing home. Margaret looked pretty good physically. She had walked for miles every day, though, and now staggered around and had to hold on to the railing. Her stories were repetitive. She was always a talker and could talk non-stop for hours. She'd always repeated herself, but now she repeated herself after just one minute. Again she told me how she had been dropped off and locked up. Again she told me. Again... Then she asked me how I was doing. I told her. Then the repetitive story started in again.

I reminded myself that feeling bad for another only locks them into their limited world. So I just smiled and told her what a lovely view she had out her window. She told me about the birds and the room. I simply tried to hold the space of love.

CHRONIC PAIN

I had plenty of practice holding the space of love, because I had done the same for my mother, who had been in chronic pain for years.

Mother had been in a great deal of pain and had some frustration and anger about it. I learned to hold the space of love: I removed my focus from her pain and frustration and pointed it instead at my love for her. It became hard for her to hold on to her anger and frustration as I held on to my love—so sometimes she let it go. Sometimes I thought the anger and frustration were mine. They were not, though; they were hers. And then they weren't even hers; they were just something she was experiencing.

DEMENTIA

My stepfather had severe dementia the last few years of his life. I believe it was Alzheimer's, but he was never diagnosed. Mother took care of him at home until the last year, when she decided to put him into an Alzheimer's unit, across the street from the assisted living duplex that she called home. They looked after him for a few hours every day so she could get a break.

We put a lock on the back door, high above his reach, so he couldn't wander out. He would sometimes go out and sit in the car. He was very angry and hateful. I think he sometimes did mean things on purpose. Mother would have company and he would reach down into his shorts/diaper and pull out some excrement and hand it to her. On one occasion her friend said, "He just did that on purpose." I don't know why he did it. But I do know he was very unhappy.

One day the administration of the clinic he had been attending said, "Why don't we just keep him here? We have an opening. He doesn't have to go home with you." And Mother said okay. He lived for another year. It was easier to dismiss the action of someone who is so far gone, than one who lingers on the edge of both worlds, like Margaret.

Anyway, this was not my first rodeo with dementia. And come to think of it, dementia is a lot like a rodeo. There are big highs and lows. And then you hit the ground. I am the clown on the other side of the barrel.

CONSCIOUSNESS SPA

A year later I asked my body, "Body, what can I do for you, to ease bringing you into the light? Are you over the relationship with anxiety?" What I heard was, "Take your body to the spa! Exercise. Take your mind to the consciousness spa and relax the mind. Meditate and dream." Our bodies talk to us constantly. My body says, "Listen to me. Ask me what I want."

"What can I do for you today?" I ask. "Rest? Exercise? Sit on the beach on the warm sand? Swim? What?"

Then I listen. Then I act. Move. Dance. Love. Eat good food. Listen to Brindl the bear. "Eat more fish!" I hear.

I listen to the whispers, so I don't have to listen to the screams. Screams turn into pain and illness. I listen and I hear, "Play. Enjoy me!" How would God talk to my body?

Never make your body wrong. Learn from it. Take your body to the spa. Take your mind to the consciousness spa, and dream.

> *Are you using your body to prove you have no choice? Or to prove how much you can overcome?*

PAIN AS COMMUNICATION

It takes a ton of energy to remain in chronic pain.

> *Pain is a message that was not willing to be received. We lock the pain into our systems. Pain is trapped ecstasy. Untrap it from your body. We won't listen to whispers. We listen to pain, in a big way. You don't need to get more conscious to heal yourself. If you are powerful enough to create disharmony, you are powerful enough to heal yourself. If you create an 'I don't like world,' then you will lock an 'I don't like world' and disharmony into your body. Instead, I'm going to relax, expand, and let go. Go into the vibration of the pain and love the vibration.*
> —RIKKA ZIMMERMAN

I took a class from Rikka in 2014, and the home play exercise was to notice what messages I got from the different things going on in my body, and what my current belief about these messages was.

My body tells me very direct things. The messages are quite literal. It's like getting hit in the head with a two-by-four. *Duh. I should have known that.*

Following is a list of beliefs and messages that I had at that time.

Knee pain

Belief: I'm injured. Not perfect. Getting old.

Message: What am I needing to do? Or have. Or be?

Stomach: burp, indigestion

Belief: I'm wrong for putting something in my body. I am

making the wrong choices.

Message: What am I not digesting?

Headache

Belief: Overwhelmed, tense, not being present. Sinus pressure.

Message: What is my head aching to do? Join with my heart? Know that I love it too?

Chest cramps

Belief: I'm dying. Why me?

Message: Where am I blocking the outpouring of my love?

Ankle lock

Belief: The joint in my ankle is locked up.

Message: Why can't I move forward?

I needed to release the beliefs and listen to the messages that I received about them. The messages were the whispers.

Pain is felt when you take yourself out of oneness.

JUDGMENTS ABOUT OUR BODIES

I also needed to release some judgments that I had about my body. I released them by answering the questions they raised.

Judgment: I am fat.

Question: What do I have too much of?

Judgment: I'm not attractive, perfect.

Question: What am I attracted to?

Judgment: I am old, and wrinkled.

Question: Where do I hang on to things? Where am I clinging and tight?

Judgment: I have a funny nose.

>Question: What smells bad or funny?

Judgment: My eyes are close together and not big. I have astigmatism and little depth perception.

>Question: What am I not seeing? Refusing to see? To what depths do I go to not see it?

Judgment: I'm out of shape.

>Question: What is the shape of things?

Judgment: My fingernails are ridged.

>Question: Where have I lined things up?

Judgment: I have high blood pressure.

>Question: Why am I always racing?

Judgment: I have an underactive thyroid.

>Question: Why can't/don't I speak my truth?

THYROID AND THROAT CHAKRA

While doing body work in 2015, I felt someone, an angel, thumping on my thyroid. On an out-breath, s/he opened up my throat chakra. I now find it much easier to speak my truth.

> *Our minds control our biology. Energy causes genes to be read in a certain way.*

LEG CRAMPS

Driving to my mom's house in 2014, with a six-hour drive to go, I got cramps in both legs.

Great, I thought. *And my drive is just beginning.*

I rubbed my legs and sent them love. I asked them the reason for the pain. What was the cramp trying to tell me? What was I being so contracted about? What was I holding on to?

There was no answer. *Whatever!* I told myself. I let it go and told myself to relax.

I pulled energy in two directions: up from the core of the earth and down from above, in the center of the universe. I pulled them through me in both directions and exploded both energies out through my legs. Then I ran some gentle energy from the universe through me. The leg cramps left.

BACK CRAMPS

Last night I had two cramps in my chest/back, on the right side and on the left. I asked why. Why am I so afraid to let love? To allow? To let go of control?

My body is trying to tell me to let go of all my beliefs and definitions. And it is doing so through contractions. It is showing me how I hold on to things.

I love me. I love my beliefs. I love the definitions of myself. Is this holding on or is this letting go? I don't know!

I think I will love the contractions, instead of judging them. I will just love them back into pixie dust. End of contractions!

You are this ever-present being that can flow through everything.

PAIN MEDITATION

I have a pain in my lower left wrist, and in the upper right wrist. What am I not "hand"ling? Or should I let go of handling? Handling, I let go of you.

Pain in the right knee. What do I "kneed"? All I need is love. Love is all I need. The Beatles' song runs through my head.

Pain in the upper back. Why am I blocking the love that is pouring through and out me? It enters through the back side of the heart chakra. Again, I am grateful to see what is going on.

Pain is a locked-in experience or emotion leaving the body. Don't hang on to the story. Feel the emotion and let it go.

> *Breathe. The re-spirit-ory system is the reset button for the spirit.*

CARPAL TUNNEL

My left wrist started hurting, just a little at first, and then more and more until I couldn't use my left hand. It wouldn't pick anything up.

Great, I thought, here I am still judging myself for my reactions.

But I did some massage therapy. I stood on my Theraplate, used my massage tool on my wrist and arm, and utilized essential oils. I took my wrist brace on and off. I asked the pain why it was there. What was I not handling?

I figured out that typing for three to four hours a day for the past month on my manuscript was a new activity that I had not been doing before, and it was aggravating my left wrist. Energetically, I journeyed to ask for help from my guides.

Three days later, it was almost perfectly normal. Isn't life funny? Pain shows us who we were, are, and who we might be.

THE EXPERIENCE OF PAIN

Pain is an experience that's meant to be released. Experience it from God presence. Being with it from the space of God Love transforms the experience.

Pain is not wrong. It's just an experience. We can't do more or create faster than God. There is no mastering of polarity in reality. Our bodies are attempting to inform us.

Release the pain body. What is the message? *Why am I not moving forward? What energy can I be instead? Let me thank my body for what it is teaching me.*

Awareness is contagious. Allow people to hurt. People need to learn their own lessons. You don't want to steal their lesson from them. You can't heal them. They can heal themselves in your presence when you hold God's love. And God is doing the healing.

AGING

I tell myself I am going to master reality by mastering aging. I think I have to overcome aging. But when we look at the lower vibrations, there is nothing to overcome.

I breathe into my being. There is nothing to conquer or override. The body is experiencing the human condition. When we see it as perfection, the experience is undone.

Molecules are pure consciousness. Aging is just a hologram. Are we allowed to defy the hologram? Defy, no. Choose, yes. We create the hologram through choice. We had to choose it for it to already be there. We chose an image.

What's the purpose of creating an image? What is our image of aging? What should that image be? Does it include wrinkles and sagging? Does a shar-pei dog care about wrinkles and sagging?

I am not a dog, you say. True, but what if your being includes the whole world? You have to do more than just participate in reality. Choose to play with reality. Leave your body alone. Your body is a miracle. Keep your cognitive mind out of it.

WHAT IF IT GETS WORSE?

"Relax into the resistance of This is not going to get any better. *What if it's going to get worse?"*
—ZACH REHDER

One of the most powerful realizations I had was around this question: What if it gets worse? With pain and illness, this is a hard one. We don't want our pain or illness to get worse. We want it to get better. That seems natural. But it can't get better until we accept it as it is. When we allow it to just be, our resistance to it disappears. Then we can love it and embrace it.

It might get worse. Yet we continue to love it. Embracing it is the next step. By embracing it, there is absolutely no resistance. There is no contraction, no trying to keep pain or illness away from our bodies. There is only embracing what is.

Then guess what? It changes on its own.

SOUND HEALING

When we make a sound, we can endure more pain. When you stub your toe, you yell. Sometimes when we are sick, we moan. It feels good to moan.

Make any sound that is not restrictive. The deepest "ooh" happens in the belly. "Aah" happens in the heart. "Ee" happens in the head. But you can bring any sound into any part of your body. It is one way to bring your heart into your head, or your head into your belly.

Try using various frequencies and your intent to heal. Tibetan singing bowls have long been used as instruments of healing.

Prayers said out loud are more powerful. And sound amplifies our prayers.

LUCID DREAM: Sound Adjustment

In 2015, I had just finished reading *A Field Guide to Lucid Dreaming* by Dylan Tuccillo, Jared Zeizel, and Thomas Peisel and I was trying to consistently have a lucid dream.

A trick I learned from the book was to stick one finger from your one hand through your other hand. If your finger from your one hand did indeed enter your other hand, you would know that you were not in this reality but in the dream world. You can do it several times throughout the day, to check whether or not you are dreaming.

So that's what I did. I asked myself, throughout the day, *Are you dreaming?* Then I checked by trying to put my one finger into my other hand. At night I asked myself, *Are you dreaming?* I put my finger through my left hand—and there it was.

And I said, *Hmmm. I must be dreaming.* There I was, in a lucid dream. Like being "awake" in my dream.

I asked for Elliot, one of my guides. Elliot showed up and brought with him someone who was shiny and handsome. I said, "Okay, now what?" Elliot said, "Listen to this. I have to adjust you with a sound wave." He gave me something like a Bluetooth, and then I could see better.

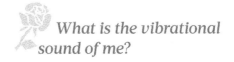 *What is the vibrational sound of me?*

MEDICINE

Take your medicine, or don't. If you want to take medicine, take it and believe in it. If you don't want to take it, don't take it. If you believe it won't work, it won't. If you believe it will work, it will.

The Placebo effect is about the power of our belief system. Are you willing to not have to prove anything? Are you willing to accept something not meaning anything? Let go of hard work, pain, and suffering. You can function from that space.

Don't give up your being for doing. It never works to figure it out—trying to figure it out just keeps you distracted. It keeps you in your mind. You need to be in your heart. Or at least in your heart/mind.

If you are infinite energy, can you give yourself the gift of Joy? Gift yourself Joy like medicine. Your awareness is a gift for those who want to return home to themselves. Gift yourself to others as if you were medicine. Gift yourself to yourself as if you were medicine. You are. For all you doctors and lawyers out there, I am not telling people to not take their medicine. I am telling them to follow their hearts as a path to Joy. Joy is also good medicine.

THE FEAR OF DYING

Let go of the feeling, *I don't want to leave.* There is no going forward or backward. There is nowhere to go. So don't worry about taking anything with you.

It is an illusion that separation exists. You are separate from separation. Ha!

You are totally supported by the universe. Live in ease. God meets you wherever you are. Fall into that energy. Let go of pain and stories of not being supported. Stand in love and love reality. Love the life you have chosen and then choose an even better one.

Talk to your body. *Beautiful body, as you release pain, you are not dying. You are safe. I have your back.*

Some say that the heart has calcifications, due to diet and life experiences. Certainly my heart has hardened with the pain of loss and grief. We love, and life changes. Those we love leave or die. We are left trying to hold on.

But the best thing we can do—for us and for them—is to be so much love that when they do leave, we wish them well on their journey.

ANIMALS AND HEALING

Rosita

Rosita was an overweight Andalusian mare. I couldn't figure out if she was mirroring me or I was mirroring her. It was the chicken-and-egg question.

Our animals often mirror us with their diseases. But it is a question that I am asking and she is not. We need to be aware of where our ideas about ourselves come from. We need to not let others project their ideas onto us, but we also need to not project ourselves onto others.

There have been many stories of dogs taking on the maladies of their owners to try to heal them. I have seen cats, dogs, and horses do this.

I hate the thought of projecting my illness onto my beloved pet. But I also don't want to take away their purpose for being here on this earth. If they take on the illness, perhaps it is their choice and purpose to do so.

I decided that Rosita would heal her thyroid when I healed mine. She would lose weight when I lost weight.

And so it was.

Olaf

We had not replaced the three dogs and cats that we had lost two years back. But we did have a cat that was visiting, Olaf. He lived with us for three years, along with his owner.

Olaf makes me smile. We have cat-sat him often since he moved out, as we are now. Olaf doesn't feel well today. I think he has absorbed some of John's stomachache from yesterday.

Olaf has a delicate stomach. So does John. I can't help but notice the pattern.

MESSAGE FROM MY SINUSES

I sat in front of the fire one day during the winter of 2015, just gazing. I asked what message my sinuses had for me.

I had chronic sinus issues. Before when I had asked, I heard, *Give up bread.* I had done this for six months and my sinuses did clear up. No headaches.

When I asked a healer some time ago about my sinus issues, she had said, "Just expand your head out to the universe." I did that, but I told myself I also had to thank my sinuses and love them as they were. But this time I asked, I couldn't hear a response. I took a deep breath. Then I heard the song from the Disney movie, *Bambi: Little April Shower.* ♫♬

What a perfect message. Every drip drop reminds me to never worry. Never hurry. Never be afraid. I continued to be reminded all day long, with every drip drop of my sinuses.

Never hurry. Never worry. Never be afraid. How exquisite our bodies are!

I have very few sinus issues now. I use peppermint oil as the weather changes. That seems to take care of it.

 Are you leaking your power?

Healing is acting in divine grace, with Love in our hearts in all that we do. God heals. We just notice it when it happens in our presence. When we hold that much love in our hearts and people are in our presence, they can't help but change. With that change, we say that they are healed.

Exercises to Heal with Love

1. To release judgment: Make a list of physical judgments you have about your body. What questions do these judgments raise? Answer the question to release the judgment.

2. To let go of limiting beliefs: Make a list of pains or physical ailments you have in your body. Then make two categories. One is your belief about the pain, and the other is a message that the pain gives you. Act on the message. Let go of the belief.

3. Say the Morning Prayer and ask to be shown what healing looks, feels, and sounds like. Ask God to show you the healing that occurs in your life. Notice where it appears in the rest of your day. Is it in your body? Your mind? Nature? In others?

*The **Bees** gift us honey.*

CHAPTER 12

Grow Abundance

*I step out into the pause. There are others, who look
like the silver water beings from the movie The Abyss.
I see three fingers rising up out of the water. There is
a gift, of a treasure chest of gold. I drink and breathe
gold coins everywhere. When I wonder what to do,
I flip a coin. I realize that true abundance is the gift
of intuition. This is the treasure in the chest. I give a
gift to the dolphins and the whales. The gold turns to
dust. A flip of the coin will always be with me. And I
will know the will of the universe.*

What is abundance? How does that relate to wealth? What do lack
and not feeling good enough have to do with it? How does worth
relate to wealth? Isn't it spiritual to be poor? How does desire factor
in?

What already matches your desire? Is it the vibration of abundance? Vibrationally, abundance is about having. You can't do that
from inside a belief system of want.

Want separates us from the universe and sets up the vibration of
wanting: the universe can't respond to want in any other way than to
continue the wanting. That's the energy of want. You can't use want
to get beyond want.

Abundance occurs when you embody the energy of having. Having eliminates the want.

*From the space of having, a
universe is born.*

Reality trains us into aligning with what doesn't work, what we want and need, instead of relying on what is working. You don't need to go down in order to go up. Don't put power into the struggle. When we feel lack, need, and want, we put power into what is. It's not about trying to be abundant, we already are abundant.

We are in a world of bad habits. You know you are graduated from scarcity when it doesn't exist. Bring in the energy of nonexistence. The biggest shift occurs with the energy of the nonexistence of scarcity. All separation goes away and all judgment. If we do find a limitation in us, celebrate it and let it go.
— RIKKA ZIMMERMAN

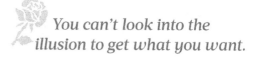 *You can't look into the illusion to get what you want.*

INSPIRED ACTION

So how do I do this? How do I experience the energy of having? I take inspired action.

"Inspired action" is a phrase that Ester Hicks uses. I like it because it differentiates busy work or distracting actions from truly helpful actions.

The mind makes you uncomfortable. The mind is uncomfortable. The higher self will lead you through the discomfort of your mind.

Ask yourself, what makes my heart sing? My answers: sacred architecture, manicured gardens, horses at play, sunrise over the water, and great food.

You are in your joy when your heart sings. Let the music in. Then you can show up from a place of joy. When your heart sings, take action. Honor your joy, and anchor more inspired actions into your daily life.

Try to see any resistance as an opportunity. Then just go through it. Fill yourself with love and overflow into the world. Be of service.

Create from the heart song. Take inspired action.

Move from the specifics of how, what, when, why, and where, to the general qualities of abundance: peace, joy, freedom, and connection. Let go of the how and ask the question, Where do I already have the qualities of abundance in my life? Share those blessings. Know that you are love, light, and infinite. Resistance is just an opportunity to push through something.

Make room to breathe. Our lives are so jam-packed. Take a breath.

OVERFLOW YOUR CONTRIBUTION

Money is an extension of the life that I love. Just last week I had a vision of myself speaking and gold coins were pouring out of my mouth.

There is a part of each of us that has never been hurt in any way. Touch that part. Anchor inner spirit, play, and contribution into your being.

In 2013, I didn't really understand that I had a contribution to give to the world, let alone how to anchor it into my being. The word "contribution" meant, to me, to give to others and not to myself. I still doubted my self-worth.

I knew that I liked to have fun and play. I now realize that my fun, play, and Joy *are* my contribution. I thought at the time that contribution had to be something serious, like healing or knowledge. It doesn't. In fact, healing isn't serious either. And knowledge? Not worth a whole lot, unless you take inspired action with it.

I also know now that until I contribute to myself, I don't have anything to offer to others.

EASE WITH MONEY

I listened to many webinars on abundance over the last few years. Money is an issue that brings out a lot of beliefs and fears in people. There is a ton of information out there on how to fix and change our financial state.

Do we have to struggle and work hard? Or can it be easy?

Prosperity is being and not doing. What are the lessons from learning, arranging, and working hard?

With ease, prosperity is complete. Ask, where am I prosperous? Expand that area. I am prosperous in my ability to love. Taste the sweetness and richness of that prosperity. Our minds are rigid and not flexible. Our minds find comfort in routine. Thank your mind. Be grateful for its default setting. Tell yourself, I am. I am...

First connect to source, and then add the content, if there is any. I find that just "I am" is enough.

—RIKKA ZIMMERMAN

I choose to make ease my ultimate priority. Easy is a choice, not a condition. I am...ease.

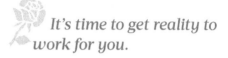 *It's time to get reality to work for you.*

LIMITING BELIEFS

In 2014 I made a list of the following limiting beliefs I held about money:

- There is lack.
- Time is money.
- We have to sacrifice.
- Worth is based on money or money is based on worth.
- It takes money to make money. We must be given the opportunity.
- Easy come. Easy go.
- Happiness does not depend on money. Or happiness does depend on money.
- Money corrupts and is the root of all evil.

I am very grateful for what I have. But I haven't equated money with gratitude.

Ester Hicks also tied money and gratitude together. In December 2014 she talked about appreciating the flow of money:

*We need to appreciate the in and the out. Not
the appreciation of the in and the guilt of the out.
Inspired spending can open the door. The more you
appreciate the spending, the more it comes back to
you. It hasn't shown up, because you notice that it
hasn't shown up. Let go of conditional wanting to
feel good.*

— Ester Hicks

A year later, in 2015, I came to realize that giving is receiving and
receiving is giving. Taking things to Goodwill is not getting rid of
stuff, but rather it is abundance overflowing through me.

> *Is your vibration around
> money the same as your
> vibration to God?*

ABUNDANCE ACTIVATORS

In 2015 I asked myself, what could I add to my life that would be
fun, joyful, and expansive and would provide infinite wealth?

As I was writing this chapter, Jack Canfield and Dawa Phillips put
out a YouTube video on the subject of abundance. It was a free video
series that spanned a three-day period. I did not take the class, but it
is sourced in the back of the book.

They asked several questions. I have answered some of their questions here. They go on to add tasks and other questions that you can
explore with them.

Following are some of their "abundance activators," and my
responses to them.

Who do I blame or praise for my current state?

If I had to, I would blame my mom for her fear. I don't blame her,
however. I don't blame anybody or anything. I hold myself responsible for everything.

At one point I blamed myself. I took on Mother's fears: of animals,
dentists, doctors, and all things mechanical. I also took on her brav-

ery, a feeling of *I can do anything.* And *I must do it myself. I don't need help from anyone.* It is a stubborn independence. I don't ask for help well and I don't receive help well.

Currently, if I blame anybody it would be the universe for placing certain conditions on me. Or myself for blaming the universe.

> *"It is easier to blame money than to take responsibility for your life. Let go of everything you think you will be if you attain it. Every belief system is about control. Money is full of belief systems. Beliefs are about automatic reactions. They create the reactions and are designed to control our behavior. We use 'this is real' to hold on to the reality.*
>
> —Rikka Zimmerman

What fixed ideas do I have?

Both Mom and Dad formed my views of money. Mother was frugal and could make do with anything. She worked hard. Nothing was just easy. From her, I learned hard work and making do. Dad was more easy come, easy go.

Dad was more easy come, easy go.

I put money into the future. Someday I will be rich. I know that I am already rich. But someday I will be richer.

Someday is in the future, though, and that tells the universe to put this in my future.

I buy a lottery ticket. I have been extremely lucky in the past. I tell myself, *Maybe today is the day.* I have hope and then disappointment.

Hope seems like a good thing to have. But when something doesn't materialize, then disappointment follows. Hope. Disappointment. Hope. Disappointment... It's an endless cycle.

If money is tied to the future, then it always exists in the future and not in the present.

What new beliefs could I seed in?

I know that basking in the total abundance of now is the only way to experience true wealth. Gratitude for what we have and are. Playing in the here and now instead of wanting or wishing for something else to occur. Wishing keeps it over there.

Where do I notice the signs of the activators in my life?

The universe will always put up a challenge. I see Coach McCarthy of the Green Bay Packers saying "Challenge," and throwing the red flag. The universe does this too. So when we find ourselves in a situation that challenges us, what do we do?

We feel the feeling that comes up: lack, lack of self-worth, disappointment, hope, destitution. We feel it until it dissipates. It dissipates when we see that love is under all things, even disappointment. We dissolve it with love and move it with gratitude. Then we take inspired action.

> *It's the doing of what you want that brings you money, not the money that allows you to do what you want.*

What are five good things about wealth?

1. Patience

   Mom had some patience. Mason, my stepfather, had none. Mason had a favorite saying: *Patience is a virtue. Catch it if you can. Seldom found in woman. Never found in man.* Sometimes I think I have the patience of a saint being married to John. Other times I think I am just playing a victim. I am saying, *See. See what I can endure. I'm righteous and you are wrong.* This is not patience but a sick form of victimhood. True patience is waiting for divine alignment. Living in the present moment minimizes the need for patience. Having said that, God moves in his own time. We have no control over the timing in life. It has more to do with trust in the future than patience.

2. Power

When I was a child, early on, I wanted to be a boy. I thought that boys had all the fun and got to do all the interesting things. Girls just played with dolls and played nurse. I hated girl games.

So I played with the boys and played boy games.

Later, as I got older, from my mother I learned the power of the woman, and soon after I learned the true nature of the balance of male and female energies. The balance of male and female energies was so much a part of my work as an architect and still is today—both as a human interacting in the world of architecture and as yin yang energies in design.

I know now that my father was very strong in appearing weak. How hard it must have been for him to do that. I had long ago forgiven him for his actions in my childhood. I had judged him as weak, and I didn't let go of my judgment until I understood that he had come into this world to play the role of weak for me. And I came on to earth to play the role of strong for him. When I realized that, I knew that power was not about weak or strong, but about balance and out of balance.

We have the belief that money is power. That we need money to be powerful. That kind of power is *power over*. Power over is not true power. There is no effort in true power. True power occurs within through just being ourselves.

3. Integrity

Mom taught me to love all beings, including animals. I grew up loving every one and finding joy in their spirit.

Attending college and trying to fit in pulled me into my head and away from my heart. It was cool to be sophisticated and have sharp retorts—not so cool to love all beings.

Integrity is now cool. Knowing who you are and allowing yourself to be it. We are all sparks from God. We are sparks of love with different individualized gifts. We simply need to discover or to remember those gifts given in love, and to mirror them back to the world so that God may know himself through us.

Integrity is knowing and staying on that path. The answer, I now know, is that the perfect world is inside of me and always has been. Integrity is knowing and acting in alignment with that knowing.

4. Pleasure

Mom taught me about the pleasure of good food and sitting with friends and talking. Playing sports and watching sports. Watching a good movie. Sitting on the couch and laughing.

John taught me about the pleasure of touch, feeling the sun on my skin, walking through a forest, gazing at the water. I taught myself the pleasure of drinking in the rays of a sunset, the sparkles off a lake, gliding across the ice on figure skates.

If we already have/are pleasure, can money buy us more pleasure? Offer us more opportunities? Yes. But not from a space of want.

5. Generosity

My mom, grandparents, and Aunt Ev were wonderful givers. I grew up surrounded by givers. John is a wonderful receiver and a good giver.

I give fairly well but I don't receive well. I don't like Christmas and presents. I feel guilty receiving gifts. As a child, I didn't feel guilty. Now I feel like I have way too much already. Two things are currently blocking my abundance: my perception of lack in the world and a lack of self-worth.

FIVE THINGS I WOULD DO WITH MORE MONEY

1. Wealth is freedom. To play however and whenever I want.

2. Wealth is influence. The greater the wealth, the greater the influence you can have on others and institutions. I would use it to help others, animals, and the earth.

3. More. More fun, more Joy, or more whatever. Just more.

4. I would travel more often and first-class.

5. I would hire more help. Cooks, construction workers, horse trainers, housekeeper—whoever might make my life more easy and fun.

If you judge people or money, you're not in a place of receiving.

FALSE BELIEFS

Where do avarice and greed come in? What Canfield and Dawa call "money wounds" and I would call false beliefs. Following are some false beliefs about money that I have held or seen played out.

Absolute power corrupts absolutely. We have to work hard for money. We have to struggle. Maybe even work in a job that we hate.

Things have a value. We have a value. We are valued and paid in accordance with that value. Money has something to do with this value.

It's Christian to be poor and give to others. To not take more than one's equal share.

It is better to give than to receive. (I am still stuck on that one.)

Money is the root of all evil. (Certainly a lot of corruption and misunderstandings have occurred around money.)

The truly spiritual give away all wealth. You can't be spiritual and wealthy. You should give all your money away to the poor.

The rich try to buy their way into heaven. Rich people despise the poor because they see them as lazy. Poor people hate the rich because they think they are evil. The poor are envious of the rich. The rich keep the poor, poor. The poor are a burden to society.

There is not enough to go around. (This is a hard one for me. I taught sustainable architecture for twenty years. I taught how the earth was becoming depleted. That it is a limited resource. This is a belief that I am still choosing to struggle with.)

None of these ideas are true. We can find anecdotal evidence that seems to show that some of them are true. We can even make them seem to be true by living in the statements as if they were laws. But it's like being an ant and crawling on an elephant and trying to discover what it is. It can't really be done.

There is something to be said for the Three Musketeers' saying, "All for one and one for all." We are all one and in one we are all. I believe in an abundant universe that supplies each according to his willingness to be supported.

I notice every day that I already am free, already have power, and know that wealth is love. Every day I have more fun. I travel. I ask for help. I am learning to receive more and more. I also help others, the animals, and the earth.

So where am I still stuck in a false belief? My mind clings to the tiniest piece of scarcity with regard to the abundance of the earth. It also allows just a little lack of self-worth to creep in. My heart knows better.

I also know that new wants will show up to replace the old ones. The universe is always showing up and asking if we want more. Of course we do. We are ever-expanding in our wants, just as the universe is ever-expanding.

Bring it in and let it go.

Frolic in your garden of abundance.

Exercises for Growing Abundance

1. List all of your limiting beliefs about abundance.

2. List ten things that are good about money . Where do you already have this in your life?

3. Where are you are not good enough or lacking in your life? Then take twenty circular deep breaths. Journal on this for fifteen minutes. Meditate for ten minutes on the perfection of your being.

4. Say the Morning Prayer and ask God to show you what abundance feels like. Ask God to show you the abundance that occurs in your life. Notice where it appears in the rest of your day.

The **Pig** *stores our wealth in his abundant body.*

CHAPTER 13

Give Gratitude

THE WEATHER

John and I had just finished natural horsemanship training at a neighbor's barn. We were in the indoor arena and getting ready to go outside to put our horses into the trailer and go home.

It wasn't far. But it was raining outside and quite slippery for putting the horses in the trailer, not to mention muddy and wet. I thought to ask my guides to stop the rain for us until we got home. But I knew that our trainer was very Christian, and I didn't want to openly offend her by inviting Gabriel and Garland to help me out. So I asked her if she had an in with the Lord and could ask for a little weather change.

She looked dumbfounded and said no, she didn't have any in with the Lord. So I thought, *Hmm... I'll just ask myself.*

"God," I said, "could you stop the rain for ten minutes so we can put the horses into the trailer, get home, and put them in the paddocks? Then you can rain all you want."

Just then the clouds opened up. Thunder crashed and all hell broke loose. It poured. I jumped and said, "Sorry, Lord. I didn't mean to offend."

I took a deep breath and we headed outside to the trailer...where it had just stopped raining. It stopped until we got home and put the horses away, and then it started again. What I thought had been an offense to God was really a "You betcha." Was that magic? Or was it gratitude and awe in prayer. I think it was a dramatic example of how gratitude, awe, and magic are interwoven.

What is gratitude? What does it feel like? How do we express it? Why is it important?

There have been many books written on gratitude. In 2012 I read *The Secret, the Magic* by Rhonda Byrne. Writing what I call "the gratitudes" each day was one of the exercises in it.

I spent one vacation on the Amtrak from Milwaukee, to Chicago, to Albuquerque, to Seattle, and looped back home by the northern route, writing down all the things I was grateful for each day. It was a good experience.

I quickly came to realize that I am grateful to be alive and here in this moment. I am grateful for every moment, especially this one. Now I am grateful that I did that exercise, because it got me to start journaling. If I hadn't done that I wouldn't be writing this book today. It was the start of my writing everything down that I thought was either a pivotal moment or simply an interesting idea. Gratitude was a catalyst for recognizing these moments.

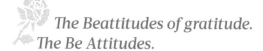

The Beattitudes of gratitude.
The Be Attitudes.

I wrote the following gratitude list at Mom's house while caring for her:

1. I'm grateful for working with essential oils.
2. I'm grateful to have time to read my book.
3. I'm grateful to spend the day with Mom.
4. I'm grateful for a nice dinner.
5. I'm grateful for the lunch out.
6. I'm grateful that a therapist works with Mom.
7. I'm grateful that Mom will get therapy at home.
8. I'm grateful that I remembered to take the garbage out.
9. I'm grateful to talk to John this morning.
10. I'm most grateful for laughing so hard with Mom. It felt so good. Thank you. Thank you. Thank you. Thank you.

Thank yous create motion.

The "you" creates movement. It gives gratitude someplace to go. Without motion, what happens? Nothing. Gratitude is stuck.

> *"Judgment is two steps behind Gratitude, which is two steps behind Love."*
> —RIKKA ZIMMERMAN

In 2014 I listened to a webcast on which Rikka discussed judgment and gratitude. I realized that first you let go of judgment of the event. Then you accept it. Then you are grateful for it. Gratitude begins the act of embracing something. And then your actions move you into love.

> *When you constantly judge you, you are becoming your awareness of the judgment around you. The judgment is not yours. It is in the environment. Get to the experience of neutral, which is zero point. Quit trying to put right on top of wrong. Move into acceptance, then approval, and then let go of the event. Go from approval, to gratitude, and then to love. Notice what you are resisting. Breathe and then embrace it. Return your whole being to love. Allow the universe to do its job.*
> —RIKKA ZIMMERMAN

Many times, I would be driving to my mom's house and the weather would go bad. It's a four-hour drive through Wisconsin winters. I would call on my guides, Gabriel and Garland, to help me out with the weather. I would say, "Would you please stop the rain or snow for just a little while until I get past the traffic in Madison?" And they would. In the next few minutes the snow or rain would stop or lessen, so that I could get where I was going, and then it would start again. As soon as it stopped, I would say "thank you."

I was grateful for what my guides had done for me. I was also in awe. I was in a state of amazement and expectation at the same time.

We can feel gratitude without amazement and expectation. It is quite pleasant. But when we add amazement, awe, and expectation, magic happens. Our expectation focuses our intent and the gratitude catalyzes the energy of our intent into motion. Voilà! Magic.

APPRECIATING WHAT IS

In 2015 I came across an Ester Hicks YouTube video on "appreciating the manifestation":

> *When I don't feel too good, I am too far away from the vibration of source. Words don't carry vibration. But they sometimes support the vibration. If I'm off the path, I know it, because it doesn't feel good. Negative emotion is guidance that lets me know that it's not what I want. I appreciate the manifestation. Revel in the expansions. Pick the best feeling disc and spin on it for a while. In the vortex, what you focus on, you see. The planet is an illusion witnessed by a particular vibration.*
>
> —ESTER HICKS

THE GET TO GAME

Mother and I used to play what we called the Get to Game. Somewhere along the way, instead of saying "I got to do this" or "I should do that," I picked up the habit of saying, "I get to do this." "I get to work out." "I get to do the dishes." I know that there will come a time in my life when I will think, *I wish I still could go work out.*

When "should" and "have to" are replaced by "get to," we change the way we feel about what we are doing. We are salt and peppering gratitude into our perception and changing a false perception into an attitude of gratitude.

I still don't love washing the dishes very much. But it does feel a little more fun. And doing this with Mom kept her in the present moment, appreciating what she could still do.

My mom was truly an amazing being. She got up every morning, the last year of her life, and said, "Thank you, God, for this day. I will do today whatever I can do." And she did.

Mom shared the Get to Game with her elderly friends. Her friends started incorporating it into their lives.

GIVING THANKS WITH ROSES

When something wonderful happens, I try to remember to say thank you, and to give my guides a rose. Giving my guides a rose seems to solidify the act of thanking them.

I love when someone gives me roses. So that's what I do, even if they are an animal guide. I gave up trying to give individualized gifts to animals—carrots, fish, or whatever it is that they eat. It was too complicated. After all, the giving of a gift is an energetic symbol of gratitude. So I give the dolphins, the bears, the birds, as well as my guides, roses.

SURFING DOWN THE WAVE OF LOVE

I had a dream about walking on water. In many of my dreams, I am standing on the shore and a huge 200-foot wave crashes down around me like a tsunami. I am always looking for a boat to get into, to be saved. In this particular dream...

> *The wave appears, but I think, Hmm. I think that I can just surf the wave with my bare feet. And I do. I surf this enormous wave with just my bare feet. Then I walk on shore and start walking up a mountain along a dirt trail. I am leading all the people from the nearby village to safety, up the mountain, away from the huge wave.*

The dream was more complicated, with the gathering of people and buildings inundated with water. But what I remember most is the transformation of fear into love, and then leading people to safety through my love. I was surfing a wave of love. The wave was merely the enormous power of God's love.

You are infinite energy. Can you give yourself the gift of gratitude?

I use the awareness door when it opens, and I walk through. I come out the other side. And then I share it. I look at other people's spirit and ask, *What do I know about this?* I harmonize as I walk through this knowing. I walk in this miracle and then let my entire being get washed in it. The negative stuff gets washed away, the limitation of others gets washed away. I say thank you as it leaves.

> *Say thank you to anything that comes up, and then good-bye.*

It's like the soak cycle on a washing machine. Then it gets rinsed away by the rinse cycle of gratitude.

It's an illusion that you're not already embodying consciousness. The reality radio station is going to continue to play. Breathe, relax, and surrender. Breathe, relax, and surrender. Breathe, relax, and surrender. I don't have to find out what I'm supposed to do. I am already doing it!

A BREATH AND A SIGH

I attended a coaching class in LA in 2016. There, I had an experience of what it was like to feel gratitude in my body.

I had recently added gratitude to my Morning Prayer. I asked the universe what gratitude felt like. I said, Universe, show me what gratitude feels like. How much gratitude can I possibly be?

Then there was a contraction in my lower sacral chakra. A gasp of wonder in through my upper body and a sigh of awe. So it was three feelings all together: contract, breathe in air, wonder, and sigh. Now gratitude seems simpler. But there is always a breath and a sigh.

Gratitude is such a powerful gift. I believe that it is the catalyst that creates magic in the world. It is the feeling that says that your intention is already on its way into your life. Gratitude lets spirit know that what is in your life is appreciated, and that spirit heard you correctly. Then spirit gives you more. When you say, "Thank you, God," God says, "You are welcome, and thank you." It is a wonderful loop and reflection of gratitude between spirit and spirit. It is inspiration.

Gratitude is the catalyst that creates magic.

Exercises for Developing Gratitude

1. Make a list of ten things you are grateful for today. What are you most grateful for? Do this for thirty days.

2. Do the Morning Prayer. Ask the universe to show you what Gratitude feels like. How much gratitude can you feel? How much Gratitude does God have for you? Listen and feel.

3. Play the Get to Game with yourself. Say "I get to do this" instead of "I have to do this." See how that changes the way you feel about what you are doing.

The **Butterfly** *flutters by and I am grateful.*

CHAPTER 14

Brew Magic

THE SHOPPING CART

It was early spring, 2014, and I was pulling into a parking space at a grocery store in Rockford, Illinois. The last traces of slush and snow were disappearing into the drainage basins. I had escaped from my mom's house to do her grocery shopping. I needed a break from taking care of her. I was frustrated about being told what to do, when to do it, and how to do everything.

I couldn't pull all the way in to the parking space because a grocery cart was in the way. I couldn't back out because a car was pulling out behind me. I was stuck. So I waited. Then I got fierce and waved my invisible magic wand at the cart and yelled at it to move. "Move. Damn it!" It didn't move. *Great*, I thought. *My magic wand isn't working. Some person could move it for me.*

And right then a man walked by, grabbed the offending cart, and moved it out of the way. I was dumbfounded.

I quickly thanked the universe for answering my request, and gave a little chuckle.

We think the universe should respond in a certain way. It always responds—but it responds in its own way.

The universe does have my back. My magic wand is working. Silly me, being hung up on how.

WHAT IS MAGIC?

What is magic? What do we mean when we say that something is magical? Does magic really exist? Are there different kinds of magic?

How does magic relate to Shamanism, Wicca, or Christianity?

To explain my answers to these questions I have written about several events that happened over the last four years, a couple of funny stories from earlier times, and some dreams of dragons, stick people, and flying saucers. I was listening to an interview on a webcast in 2012, when the guest mentioned that Arcturus was the spirit of architecture. And Noden was the spirit of healing. I had not heard of either before, and thought I should do some research on them. I opted for direct connection.

> *I contacted both spirits. Arcturus was not clear. He was a Greek man with curls of blond hair. I asked him for help on the Ryan Park project, a nature center that I was working on. A spirit horse reared. Then Noden, an old man, stuck me in the eye with his stick. I keep getting stuck in the eye with a stick. You'd think that I would just learn to open my eyes.*
>
> *I said good-bye to the spirit horse and threw him an apple. Then I rode back down on a rainbow of pixie dust. I had gossamer wings. It was so light and so wonderful. What a beautiful ride.*

I came back to Mother's house to take her to therapy. She was dressed up and ready to go.

I decided to research Arcturus on the web. I found a lot of information about a very bright orange star in the Bootes, architecture firms, bands with that name, and an organization for social architecture which advocates the creation of a better world through the clarification of what we really want. Nodens (Nudens, Nodons) is a Celtic deity associated with healing, the sea, hunting, and dogs. He is equated with the Roman god Silvanus. Interesting, because our farm is called Silver Creek Farm.

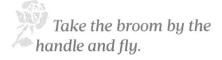 *Take the broom by the handle and fly.*

SPOON BENDING

In 2014, I attended an animal communication class with Asia Voight. During breakfast one morning I was talking with some friends about the session that was going on. They had attended the previous class, but I had been unable to attend because Mother was recovering in the hospital at that time. I had missed the spoon-bending exercise they had done and was disappointed, because it was one of the things that I was looking forward to. They told me that they had both bent their spoons and that they would be willing to show me how. We went to their hotel room. I brought a very stiff spoon to practice with, from the breakfast table at the hotel.

They had an entire ritual around the bending. It seemed Japanese in origin. We awakened the meridians in both arms and hands, up and down, from our heads to our hearts. We repeated "May the light be in me" three times. Then we said "Hai" ("Yes") moving and clapping our hands in a circle, both clockwise and counter-clockwise, about ten times.

Then I tried to bend my spoon. It wouldn't budge. I tried and tried. Still it wouldn't move. One of the women bent her spoon. I watched. She took my spoon and bent it too. And then she bent it back.

I gave up trying and then took a deep breath and let out a sigh. Then I bent my spoon. It turned into melted butter in my hands. And it bent—this spoon that was so stiff that I couldn't possibly bend it with all my strength. I ran around the rest of the day with my spoon in my hand. I showed it to everybody. I was so pleased with myself. I now keep the bent spoon in my pencil holder on my desk. It reminds me of what is possible when we let go of trying and just allow. Or as Yoda would say, "Don't try, do. Do, or do not."

RIGHT AND WRONG VS. INFINITE POSSIBILITIES

In 2015 I considered the concepts of right and wrong versus the concept of infinite possibility. I normally stay out of the belief system around right and wrong. I tell myself to embody the field of infinite possibilities.

I embody the unified field. This is the same energy as bending a spoon, manifesting a bowl of strawberries, walking through walls, and bilocating. When walking through a wall, you are so much a part of the wall that it is not separate from you. So of course you can walk through the wall. I am the glitch in *The Matrix* like Neo, and I invite the world to infinite possibilities.

When we encounter magic or a cosmic coincidence, the event shatters the edges of our belief structures. If it is small, it tickles at the edge of us. If it's significant, it may shatter the entire belief.

Of course, we come up with new replacement belief structures. We always do. Our minds are forever active and always need something to concoct. Hopefully the new beliefs we make are more expansive and inclusive. We spiral upward and return around. There's a new belief. Turn around. New belief. It is never-ending, in an upward spiral. That is why it sometimes seems as if we aren't getting anywhere. But our new way of being is just becoming commonplace. We don't see that we have risen, in addition to returning around. Thank you, Magic, for tickling and blasting away at our constructs.

> *Different versions of people show up in different dimensions.*

Magic, to me, is something that science hasn't yet been able to explain. But I also think of it as something that is fun and sparkly and full of unicorns and pixie dust. To me that is also magical.

RITUAL MAGIC

There are magicians out there who practice magic. There are Wiccans who perform spells, speak words of power, and perform rituals. That is one definition of magic.

The druids who walked the earth long ago and spoke to nature engaged in a kind of magic. The shamans of many native cultures and also the modern urban shamans engage in the direct revelation of source, another kind of magic. Sometimes priests and rabbis from institutionalized religions have experiences that offer divine revelation. That too is magical.

I classify all of these as ritual magic, because most of these occurrences are the result of a ritual performed and handed down by a formalized institution or group.

When I was twenty, I played with Wiccan magic. I bought books, read about spells, and tried some. I tried to perform some rituals. "Tried" is the key word. Ritual and words can have great power. Ritual focuses the mind and body. With focus comes power. If belief is there also, then magic can happen. For me, the ritual was too much work and somewhat boring. I just wanted to say a thing and have it be so. Many Wiccan rituals end with the words "And so it is." For many, the ritual is necessary. The ritual of the Catholic Church is a good example. I think it's too bad that they gave up on their ritual and Latin words. I think those words had power. Power is lost trying to entertain understanding.

SHAMANISM

At some point, I gave up on magic as defined by Wiccan rituals, and I turned to Shamanism. I read many books about it.

The appeal was the direct revelation and direct experience of source, but without the trappings of organized religion, though it did have the trappings of various culturally laden schools of thought. It had lots of practices that seemed strange and were difficult to do without living in a far-off place devoid of people. I read about them but had no shaman to help me on my path and felt alone. I hid my studies—I didn't want people to think I was crazy—but I continued to read and dabble in the Toltec ways.

CHRISTIANITY

I was raised a Presbyterian and consider myself a Christian. I believe in Jesus Christ. I carry him in my heart. I have wept at his feet and asked him, Why have you forsaken me? I have walked hand in hand with him in joy. I have seen God from a distance, and felt the power of God, just an inkling, run through me. That direct experience too was magical.

HEALING

I decided that I would become a psychic healer, so I read everything I could get my hands on about healing. I tried a little reiki. I liked working with animals better than working with people. They were much easier and more receptive. Also, they don't lie. They may play around with you, but they don't lie.

So I started to play at healing animals, and I decided that animal communication would help. I began to read books about animal communication and took a few courses. I discovered that the internet had lots of webcasts by people offering what I wanted to learn. I began taking courses. And my spiritual development rushed forward in great bursts. I talked to animals, spirits, guides, the earth, rocks, the universe, Jesus, the wind, the sun, teachers, and friends. All have given me counsel.

WISDOM

I learned that I was always a healer. I discovered that I had wisdom to share—or, rather, I was reminded of it. My mother had told me that I was born with wisdom, and that at the age of nine I was already wise. I had always hung out with adults and listened to them talking. But I also knew that I didn't want to grow up and be one of them, because they didn't have any fun.

I knew what people were feeling. I could read their bodies. All I had to do at this time was to quit hiding. My writing this book is me coming out of hiding. Even if no one ever reads it, I will have written it. And I am no longer hiding.

THE CHICKENS

This is a very funny story. In its own way it is about magic.

John was an agricultural volunteer in the Peace Corps. Back then there were only two kinds of volunteers: English as a second language (TESL), or agricultural volunteers. He was an "ag volunteer" and I was a TESL volunteer.

John's job was to introduce animal husbandry in the form of chickens and pigs to the people on Imroj, Jaluit, in the Marshall Islands. The local people were familiar with chickens and pigs. They ate them at celebrations. Chickens ran free on the island until some young drunk man decided to eat one late at night, or there was a party, and then the chickens were all gone. The idea was to introduce animal husbandry, so that there would be plenty of chickens and pigs to supplement the fish diet.

John spent a couple weeks building a chicken coop to put his chickens in. The coop was a work of art. It was raised up on stilts, had slanted decorative frond sides, a thatched roof, and a ladder that allowed the chickens to walk up to the raised platform and enter. It was high off the ground, to be out of reach of the wild dogs, cats, and vermin.

Every morning John let the chickens out to eat grubs and bugs. He ground up a concoction of ground coconut, fish heads, rice, and *jubup en banana*, the center shoot of a banana tree, and fed it to the chickens. It took hours to prepare. Even grating coconut is a chore when you do it with a *kein ranki*, a crowbar-type device mounted to a tree stump that acts a stool. After a few weeks, we noticed that every night at sunset, a group of men would gather outside our grass house. There was a path up the middle of the atoll, lined with white-painted stones on both sides. The men sat on the edge of the sidewalk on the rocks, laughing and talking. After a few weeks, John asked them why they were there and what they were talking about. It took a while to learn enough language to be able to ask the question.

They said that they were there to watch the magic. "What magic?" John asked.

They replied, "Well, every night your chickens climb up the stairs and go into your little house and we want to see what magic spell you put on them to do that."

John was taken aback. He laughed and said that there was no magic spell. He explained that he just fed them every night at sunset and they went into the coop to sleep.

"Why do you feed them? We don't feed chickens. Chickens feed us," they said.

"I feed them because they are in a coop, and they need more food than they can find."

"We don't feed them. They feed us," they replied.

And so the discussion of magic and agriculture went. In order to get chickens from the agricultural department in the district center, they had to build coops. When they did, they didn't want to feed the chickens or let them out. All the chickens were eaten at a party at Christmas time anyway.

After that, there were no chickens, in or out of the coops.

What is the moral of the story? Don't import any chickens before Christmas in the Marshall Islands. It's also about our perception of magic. Magic is merely seeing something that is unexplainable. Everything is truly magical if we choose to see it that way.

MAGIC PRACTICE

I did the same exercise with magic in 2015 that I had previously done with gratitude. Every day for a month I wrote down a list of all of the magical occurrences that I saw in my life.

At first it was a series of what some people would call cosmic coincidences. There were a lot of those in our life and they certainly seemed magical. Then I began to appreciate seemingly ordinary things as also magical. I wrote about the workings of the body and the songs of the birds and the rustle of the leaves on the trees. The crickets and birds singing with John when he played his guitar. The ducks on the pond laughing when we told a joke. Many simple things can be seen as magic, as well as the truly extraordinary occurrences in our lives that some people call miracles.

FLYING SAUCERS

In 2015, I had a very active dream, probably due to eating too much redfish and then going to sleep.

> *I was standing with a group of people looking out a window and I saw a bright blue light shaped like a pyramid on its side in the sky. On the end of the pyramid was a flower design. I asked the people standing next to me, "Do you see that?" They said, "No." "You don't see that bright blue spaceship-like light? It almost looks like glass." "No, we don't see it," they said.*
>
> *A little to the left were several circles of many lights, like a wreath of lightbulbs, with four lights in*

the middle like a square. I said, "Do you see those lights that are moving?" "No," they said. "We don't see those either."Hmm, I thought. Then several of the circular lights were moving in our general direction. Then several small, flat circular lights hung outside the window. "How about those? Do you see those?" I asked. They looked about the size of plates. Yes, they did see those.

Then one of the light saucers flew into the room and entered my heart. It split my heart open and my whole body seemed to explode. I said to the people, "Let's get out of here."

"Let's just go through the wall," I said. "We will be okay."

We went through the wall and came out into a beautiful yard. I said, "Well, the last time I had this dream I hid in the ditch, and they didn't get me. So let's do that." I then saw a woman with two dogs who was also running from the light. I said, "You saw them too and you ran last time." She said "yes."

I woke up then. I realized that the spaceship was blue crystal and that I should not have run. There was no reason to be afraid. Next time I will accept the light without fear. Or at least hope I will. Who knows what will happen in dreamtime?

 *Dreams are our creation.*

FEAR ACCELERATES MAGIC

In November 2016, I had a dream....

I was very magical. I walked through walls and I was very powerful. People were pursuing me because I was so powerful. I was afraid and wanted to hide. I decided I would hide in a table. I would become a table and sit outside on a patio. I thought that the person looking for me wouldn't see me. He would just see a table.

I became the table and looked out through the table's eyes. I saw the person looking at me. He didn't notice me, but as I stared at him, he began to see me, until his eyes met my table's eyes. I thought to divert my eyes so he wouldn't make contact. But it was too late. He had discovered me.

So I decided to become a tree growing outside the patio. Surely he wouldn't notice an ordinary tree just growing there. But once again he did notice me. He saw my tree's eyes looking out at him.

I left in a hurry, flying away, and woke up.

The next evening, during Rikka's weekly class, I thought about my dream. In fact I thought about it all day. I concluded that I needed to be so powerful that, even if I was discovered, I could stand in my power openly, and then no one could ever hurt me. I saw the small girl, Drew Barrymore, in the movie version of Stephen King's *Firestarter*, blasting flames against her pursuers. And I decided I had to be that powerful. But I also knew that I wouldn't hurt anyone as she had. I would just stand in my power, unafraid, knowing no one could hurt me. That was my first realization.

Listening to the class, I thought, *I should be so much love that a bubble would form around me, which nothing could penetrate. Bullets and missiles would just drop away and they would be transformed by the love. The bullets would fall to the ground, entering my space. I would stand in the power of love.*

Then I realized that the person staring into my table eyes was really me, my own fear rearing up to keep me hidden from my own magic. No people. No pursuers. Just my own fear.

I didn't need fire or love bubbles to protect me. I was already safe. I didn't need to create missile objects out of fear. The fear wasn't even mine. The fear belonged to the environment of the world we live in. It could simply stay there.

I don't need to have fear in order to protect myself. Fear just makes bullets and missiles. Bullets can't exist inside of love. I will be and am the center of love. And I choose to share it with the world through my magical being.

The act of becoming a table was most magical, and I was flaunting it in the face of fear. This was an act of bravery, and also an act of pure fun and joy, which is what I felt. It is fun to become wood and look out through the eyes of a table! You are absolutely frozen in space, and so still. What is it like to be a tree? In place also but with rustling leaves and sunshine and wind and swaying and breathing, rooted through the ground and drinking water and absorbing minerals and transforming them into bark and so much more.

I would never have decided to become a table without fear pushing me to do it. I might have chosen a tree, though. Living things that breathe are much more interesting to me.

DRAGON DREAM

One morning in 2016, I went into my Morning Prayer. I chose to be with both magic and divine perfection, to see the perfection in magic and the magic in perfection.

And then I noticed that the rain had watered my brother-in-law Jim's plants. I had potted them the day before and placed them outside without watering them. They needed water. So the rain was for him and me, perfection. I was noticing my gratitude for the rain, and then my gratitude led to magic.

Staring into the morning fire, I think of dragons. I am reminded of Sedona, where dragons took on a special meaning for me. As I stared into the fire...

> *I stand on the stage in Sedona, all my friends are in the audience. Brindl the bear, saying, "You are sweet like honey." "No, I'm not," I say. "Yes, you are," he says. "Not a bone in my body," I say. "You are," he says. "Okay, I am."*
>
> *I hang my head down and sigh, take a deep breath, continue on. The dolphins are leaping in the audience. They are about laughing and the joy of playing.*

They giggle and run on their tails backward as they leap and cavort. I smile at their exuberance.

Of course, Pegasus is also there. He is my soul support. He is my land dolphin. Phoenix is there too low down and to my right, red in his magnificence. "Out of the fire and chaos. In the center is the quiet." Hold to the center to remain quiet is his gift. Bluebird sits on my left shoulder as always, chirping, "Be happy. Be happy. Be happy."

Garland is there. She looks like the garland on a Christmas tree, gold in color. She has never incarnated. Gabriel is there and all of the guides and friends of the audience. The audience is there. I acknowledge their presence.

Rikka and Nikole are also there, as is Rikka's monkey and Nikole's whale, Uva. I find it a cosmic joke that Rikka has a monkey on her back! I laugh.

Once I have greeted everyone, I set out on a journey. Today's journey is with dragons. We have journeyed many times. But today we glimpsed the heart of God.

I begin sharing the journey by walking down stone stairs into the dungeon, which lies beneath the castle. It is where the dragons live.

The dungeon becomes a cavern. I turn right to exit the cavern and exit out onto a meadow. The meadow is green, with wild flowers, and there's a blue sky with no clouds. There are trees in the distance, a forest. To the left is a cliff. All of the dragons are lined up in a horseshoe on the outskirts of the meadow. There is a dragon for each of us, a dragon for every member of the audience and for each person reading this.

I explain that dragons are able to go between, anywhere and anytime. They are saddled and we can hop on. We must walk out to meet them halfway. Then they will meet us the other half. They will choose us. We can then greet them and have a conversation. If we are timid, we can sit on a nearby bench and simply get to know them. If we are brave, we can hop on and soar.

I hop on. We go to the edge of the cliff and jump off. We soar.

I ask my dragon where he would like to go. What would he like to share? I invite the others to do likewise.

My dragon is a she. Her name is something like Eehs Koocha. She is gold and somewhat small. She has ruby-red eyes and an emerald-green diamond star on her forehead. She tells me her true name, which should not be repeated. She also has a common name. When we learn a true name we can join our hearts with their heart. Her heart joined mine.

I saw power and humility juxtaposed into a form of yin yang. Power and humility flowed back and forth—absolute power arising out of the center of humility and then absolute humility arising out of the center of power.

And then I saw a glimpse of God. OMG. It was ever so fleeting and nothing that could ever be held on to. A glimpse.

I walked into the kitchen and had a drink of water. As I stood looking out the kitchen window, I morphed back into the heart of the dragon.

I saw what she saw. Through her eyes I saw a kaleidoscopic world made up of ever-changing facets of color, like one sees when looking through a kaleidoscope. One small turn, and the world changes. And this is how a dragon goes anywhere at any time. He just chooses one of the facets and then enters that world. He blinks his eye and the facets change. The world changes. So that is how a dragon travels. He merely changes the world.

I can't hold on to the morphs. They are a million in a second. They fire at me like frozen frames from a film strip slowed down in time. Then they speed up even more. I can notice them but cannot morph unless they are still enough for me to hook onto them. I explain this to the audience. They throw all their guides and power animals at me. Some of them I morph into and notice. Others I will play with later. For now I am with the dragon.

I thank my dragon. I give her a rose. The rose goes up into the air and I am showered with petals. I ask and know that, as always, my path will be strewn with rose petals so that I may know my way. I can see it. I can smell it. It gives new meaning to "Stop and smell the roses." I love that. I love my dragon. I love the world. I love God.

Magic and divine perfection, what wonderful words to notice and play with today! All this came from my Morning Prayer.

DREAM OF STICK PEOPLE

Last night, November 2016, when I went to sleep, I asked that my dream be a lucid dream. That I remember it and that it be magical. I asked to learn about energy and seeing and perhaps healing. I didn't want my sleep time to be wasted.

This morning I woke up, and I thought, *Hmm. Nothing. That's disappointing.* Then I thought about it a little more.

I was flying around and landing in the trees and saw some stick people. I saw a person who was made of sticks and a beast who was made of sticks. My first reaction was that they might harm me and I would have to fly away. Something was chasing me and I went through a building and then flew over an ancient city, flying low and between the buildings. I was no longer being pursued.

I created, with my fear, an image of being chased. When will I quit getting in my own way? Some time ago, I told myself, "Whenever I find myself flying in a dream, I will awaken in that dream." I didn't last night, though.

But if I think about it, it certainly was magical. Was there any healing? The healing is that I let go of the fear that I was creating. The magic is that we turn our emotions into images, events, and stories. In the same way that God created us in his image, we create reflections of our feelings.

So be careful with what you feel. Feel it. Don't suppress it.

DRAGON DRIVE

In December 2016, I drove into Green Bay to get some body work done. I was listening to a recording of Rikka's class from the previous week. I was driving along...

And then I found myself talking to Rikka, who was positioned outside of my car, just outside my windshield. I thought, Hmm. And I just kept driving. I had a conversation with her about dragons and how I had been morphing into dragons recently. Then...I morphed into a dragon.

I turned the recording off. I thought that perhaps driving, talking to Rikka, being a dragon, and also listening to Rikka on my car stereo was just too much. I felt the dragon throughout me. I looked out and felt huge. I breathed out and fire came out. I breathed out and fire came out again. That's interesting, I thought. I felt my wings flap—or undulate, more than flap—and off I flew.

And yes, I was still driving my car to Green Bay.

I asked if there was a message the dragon wanted to share. I heard, Dragon wisdom and dragon power.

Fire transforms. The dragon transforms with his fire and power. I have the fire, passion, power, and strength to transform myself and others. That is the message.

MAKE BELIEF

When children play, we call that make believe. Isn't that interesting? What if when children play, they are just making their beliefs come true? What if that is the true nature of magic? That we make our beliefs come true. We believe them so much that they become a knowing. A knowing is already true.

I enjoy my dragon visions. Is shapeshifting real? Is it true? When we make believe, we make it real. It is true and it is magical.

Quit calling daydreams fantasy.

Exercises for Brewing Magic

1. List ten things that happened today that you consider magical or cosmic coincidences. Do this for twenty-one days.
2. Do the Morning Prayer. Ask God to show you how much Magic you can be. How much Magic is in your life? How much Magic does he see in you? Notice the Magic that happens in your day.

The Unicorn flies and the Dragon breathes fire.

CHAPTER 15

Explode into Bliss

Bliss is not something that can truly be described. It exists in the crown chakra and above, in an unknowable place that just exists so that we can experience space and time, and experience feelings across space and time.

Although Bliss is indescribable, it can be experienced. I will attempt to share my experiences of what I only call Bliss for lack of any better word.

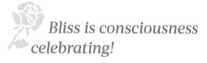 *Bliss is consciousness celebrating!*

NOT IN HAWAII: EXPLOSION

In June 2014 I attempted to join the group in Hawaii from afar. This was a multidimensional being class that I couldn't attend because I was taking care of Mom. This was the second time that I joined this class. The first time was discussed in the chapter on Harmony. My reaction to this meditation was OMG OM Me.

I did some deep breathing and relaxed my body. I ran healing discs of color through my body, as if I was on a gurney and they were hoops of color that passed over me like in an MRI. There was one color for each chakra and some extra ones in silver, gold, and pink. By the time I finished ten colors, I was very relaxed.

Then I ran energy through my being for two hours, spiraling up and down, clockwise and counter-clockwise. I reached high into the heavens and down into the earth. And then...

I had a central sun explode out of my heart that was as big as the universe. I did the "You are light, you are love, and you are infinite" meditation. I did fifteen seconds of breathing in and out.

To say I experienced bliss doesn't do justice to what I felt and saw.

The white light and colors were incredible. Every cell in my body was vibrating and going to explode. I gave up control and allowed.

THE BEGINNINGS OF NOTICING

Later, I experienced bliss again. I went there immediately. I did the "You are love, you are light, and you are infinite" meditation to the walls.

Everything around me changed into light. I am beginning to allow. I have noticed that I don't have to reach up for source. The source is within.

I was beginning to notice that I don't have to try. The highest vibration is already within, and I simply need to notice it. "Need" is too strong a word. Rather, it's a pleasure to allow my noticing of it.

CHIROPRACTIC ADJUSTMENT

In Costa Rica in February of 2015, I did breath work every day at 7 a.m., for five days. I did my morning meditation before this, at 5:30, as the sun rose. I journaled the following description of the breath work:

My crown and third eye chakra had an immense vibration. It was as if a huge iron bar was moving through my body and vibrating. A large area over the throat chakra was vibrating, but it was repressed. I had the experience of seeing angels, Mom, and Stacy. There were a lot of body adjustments. Pain. Breathe. Gone. I remembered when I used to breathe through pain to heal it long ago. But this was more of an acknowledgment of it.

When I went to get up, I rolled over on my side and pressed the bottom several vertebrae in my lower back. The vertebrae were sucked back into place. I was amazed at how I knew just where to press. I had an entirely different body. I was so much more flexible. I could remember feeling that way a long time ago—it was me returning to myself. I had tears in my eyes when I rolled over to get up.

Once I let the grief out, the Joy simply emerged. Joy didn't come into me from the outside. Joy emerged from inside of me and spread out.

KEYS TO THE UNIVERSE

I breathed circularly for thirty minutes and then fell in...

I saw angels and aliens, my mom and my horse. They were golden and there were many energy beings. I walked briefly among them, smiling and happy to be there. The breath moved through me as if through a tube. The breath was breathing itself. I saw my breath as a jellyfish, circular and in three dimensions. I continued to breathe. I saw porpoises grinning. Then I was a porpoise grinning. Breathe. People around me doing breath work were laughing and crying and screaming. And joyful.

I was at peace and wondered if I should go on one of their journeys. But no. That was their journey, not mine.

We should breathe together. We were breathing together. We and the universe were all breathing together. So I was not keeping them out, but breathing them all in. It was a vibrational symphony.

I saw Jesus. And then there was total blackness. Shouldn't I see light? A light shone down on me like I was under the spotlight of God. Then I realized that the light was coming out of me and I was the source of the light. God was the breath running through me. He was with me every time I took a breath.

A small pain or ache happened here and there. Left hip, right knee. I noticed and thanked the universe for pointing out the contraction. I breathed through it, loved it, and looked elsewhere. Then I noticed that the pain had left with my gratitude.

I had deep stomach contractions. My body arched up. I noticed and I started to cry. But crying wasn't necessary. I noticed the contractions, relaxed, and breathed through them.

There was a deep pain, high and on the right side in my back/shoulder. I felt as if I was levitating high, leading with my chest. I had cramps on my right side. I breathed and relaxed.

Rolling onto my left side, I gently cried. I felt as if I had been given the keys to the universe.

Editing this now, I notice the breath of God running through me again, and am overwhelmed by a rolling contraction and tears and joy all at the same time. Isn't it wonderful to know that all we have to do is notice the breath of God? It is there with every breath we take.

SUFFERING ISN'T MANDATORY

A unicorn put his horn in my third eye and it opened. Then Pegasus entered me and said, I am Pegasus, and we flew off. I was in bliss...just noticing.

On the left I saw wriggling humanity. It looked like a scene from Dante's Inferno, with a lot of slithering. They were suffering over there. None of it was necessary. I was simply noticing.

There were screams and laughter all around in the room where we did the breath work. The sounds joined with the bird calls outside. We were not separate from the screeches of the birds. It was a symphony of sound all around. But it was entirely peaceful here, noticing.

I saw Jesus on the cross, not suffering, truly being beyond suffering. Humanity doesn't have to suffer. They choose to.

I'm simply floating. I'm going here and going there. A pain appears. More stomach contractions. A sadness almost appears. But then there is nothing. I completely relax, breathe, and open up. I relax the body, and then there's a contraction.

> *Success is feeding the soul with vibrant energy. And living in the overflow.*

THE BLISS BOMB

I had a vision in March 2015, while staring at the fire in my fireplace. The fire is such a good place to lose one's mind during the winter months in Northern Wisconsin. You can't come to your senses until you've lost your mind!

Andi was standing behind a bar in Pagosa Springs, Colorado. She was serving up the specialty of the house, a Bliss Bomb.

This was the name she called herself in Costa Rica, where I met her. She was dressed in black mesh stockings and an Old West barmaid's outfit, complete with push-up bra.

"Step right up," she said. "Get your Bliss Bombs here."

Or you can have a shot of giggle juice. Sprinkles of pixie dust. Or an infusion of green earth nectar. For the more citified folk she serves up lattes with sprinkles of love with their cinnamon. Cookies are guaranteed to bring smiles and chocolates are advertised to be orgasmic. People are lined up in the streets to drink at her bar.

She passes her hand over the Bliss Bomb as she hands

it to the customer. It bubbles and foams pink, spilling over the rim and onto the counter. The customer is transported to another world. A world of Bliss.

LIGHT BEINGS

Last night I saw light beings while engaging in breath work.

There were billions of lights, which became stars. The stars morphed into light beings. The beings swirled and massed around a central core. I wondered if that central core was God. Then they showed me that it was me. And that they all loved me. I thanked them, gave them a rose, and they showered me with rose petals.

You are not your awareness. You are what you do with your awareness.

ENLIGHTENMENT

In June 2015, I saw...

A whirling around the body. And then? What? Enlightenment? Okay. What could be easier? There was a subtle movement of the outside energy layer. And then there was a buzzing.

I shared this experience with people but they didn't seem to care. I was a step into another dimension. Viki, a friend, asked me if I could bring the experience into the here and now. And so now I do.

SCRAMBLED TIME AND SPACE

When space becomes an eternity and time is everywhere, you see I have scrambled time and space into scrambled eggs. It is something to be eaten with toast, butter and jelly. When you take a taste, you see light and darkness. Joy is sprinkled with sadness. Ecstasy with pain. Peace with excitement. A brief moment of terror with utter calm. All at once and at the same time, in a linear fashion.

And then the moment that lasts an eternity is over, and you are here and now. So what do you do now? I have chosen to share it.

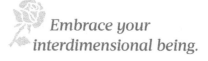

Embrace your interdimensional being.

Exercises for Exploding into Bliss

1. Do the Morning Prayer. Ask God to show you what Bliss feels like. Ask God how much bliss you can possibly be. Can you see it, feel it, taste it, or hear it? Make sure you start with a great deal of gratitude. The gratitude will turn into Joy, which turns into Bliss.

2. Let go of control. Let go of any definition you have of bliss. Allow whatever shows up. Embrace it. Show gratitude.

3. Relax your body. Ground it. Run hoops of color up from your feet, as if they were a fine mesh. Each one a color of their chakra and each one becoming more refined. Go from your feet up over your head. Add a couple extra hoops that are pearlescent in pink, gold, and silver. When you are relaxed, grounded, and the energy is moving, say *I am love, light, and infinite.* Then notice.

The **Lightning Bug** *glows into the night.*

CHAPTER 16

Speak the Truth
UFO

In February 2016, I was in Bimini attending a Life Transformed Coaching retreat for the week. One day in the early afternoon, we chartered a boat to chase after dolphins. The seas were very rough, almost too rough to go out in. We were looking for a place to swim with a pod of dolphins, excited by the possibility of being in the water with one of God's very sacred creatures.

The boat crashed against the wind for two hours. No dolphins. Eventually the boat stopped in a relatively calm location to let a few people swim around and get wet. I stayed on board and stared out at the sea. I was comfortable in my seat with my feet up.

After a while, as people were getting back on board, a butterfly fluttered by me and over my left shoulder and then out to sea. It was a white flutterby (as I like to call them). They had a local name too; it was something like *money bot*. They were supposed to bring good fortune to those who saw them. I wondered how a flutterby got to be out in the middle of the sea. Maybe it hitched a ride when we took off.

I continued gazing out at the ocean. People were still moving around.

Then I noticed a plane out in the distance, not too far away. I watched it for a while, but it didn't move. It didn't go left; it didn't go right. It didn't go anywhere. it just stayed there hanging in the sky like a cigar.

I asked my friend, "Nikole, do you see that?" I pointed out the airplane. "It's not moving."

She looked and said, "No, it isn't. It looks like a ufo."

We watched it. Christine approached and asked, "What are you looking at?"

"There's a ufo," I answered.

"Where?" asked Christine. "I don't see it." And then, "Oh, I see it."

We watched the object, which was still not moving. And then it wasn't there. And then it was. And then it wasn't. And then it was gone. There was no sound. It just flickered out of space. But before it did, I managed to ask "them" if they had anything to say. I heard: "See you later."

There were no clouds. It was a perfectly blue sky. People finished getting on board. We left for another location.

I thought it was significant that the incident was heralded by a white flutterby. I had recently learned a lesson from watching a flutterby. I told the flutterby that it should come to me and sit on my finger.

I paused. And I listened. Then I said "No, I will not try to control you. I will just enjoy your presence as you flutter by."

So the flutterby had taught me the lesson of enjoying what I see without trying to control it. I learned that you can't hold on to anything and that you can only appreciate it when it is in front of you. You can't make a flutterby stay with you. You can only enjoy its beauty as it goes on its way.

You can't hang on to Joy. You can only enjoy the present moment. Hanging on puts you in a state of contraction and then the Joy is gone. Lately butterflies had appeared to me several times. It was like they were saying, *Pay attention. Something interesting is about to happen.*

THE TRUTH OF THE MATTER

What is Truth? Can it be defined and still be truth? Can we differentiate between the truth and science of the 3-D world and the Truth of spirit in the fifth dimension? Are we all just players on Shakespeare's stage, *full of sound and fury signifying nothing?* How do judgments and awareness relate to Truth? Is there one great Truth?

Knowing is a truth, while beliefs are just illusions that trap us into limitations and judgment with a story. I have given some examples of how to let go of fixed positions and empty the energetic trash. When the trash is empty, what we are left with is the Truth.

> *"Words are at best an honest lie."*
> —RIKKA ZIMMERMAN

HONEST LIES

This book is for me. I know that now as I type these words. This book is for me. It doesn't matter if anyone else reads it. It is the act of writing it that is bringing everything through me.

I try to separate the past from the present as I see the past through my current understanding, which isn't the same as it was even a minute ago. One foot is in the past. One foot is in the present. My mind is in the past and my heart is in the present. I have to write with my heart flowing through my mind, or maybe with my mind flowing through my heart. Which way it flows doesn't matter. It only matters that my heart and mind are combined. Only then can I have a chance of telling the truth.

> *In a meditation, a unicorn reamed out my throat chakra with his horn. He then said, "Whisper and just listen."*

We have the saying, "if truth be told," but truth can't be told. I won't judge myself for trying. Words, in and of themselves, are limitations. They are a perspective of something. They necessarily limit what we are describing by putting the idea into a box. A tree is green. And yet it is so much more.

I am currently reading Deepak Chopra's *The Third Jesus*. In it he explores the teachings of Jesus. I think, *If Jesus can't or didn't explain the truths of God to people in a way that they could understand, how can I expect myself to do an adequate job of explaining the truth?* So I let myself off the hook.

> *Recalibrate the heart and mind to truth.*

WAKING DREAM

I had a dream last night.

> My toes were each on fire, like they were individual candles. Then the last two baby toes were really lit up.
>
> I was sitting in a chair looking at them after a massage. I wanted to meditate. I was wondering if I had a cold. Two people got me some cold pills. I had a vest on that belonged to the masseuse. She wanted it back.
>
> I didn't want to take the cold pills because I wanted more clarity. But I did take them. And then I woke up...

Or did I really just go to sleep? I took the pills and then woke up, asleep. When we are awake, our mind is active. When we are asleep, our heart is active. It's the age-old question: Am I a person dreaming that I am a butterfly, or am I a butterfly dreaming that I am a person? Am I a sleeping person dreaming that I am awake? Or am I an awake person aware that I am sleeping? We are both.

WAVE ENERGY

I've been seeing energy for years. I see energy flowing out of people's hands and mouths as they speak. Energy around trees and animals. Colors and interactions. *Okay, so you see energy,* I tell myself. *So now what?* I thought that if I saw the world as energy, then I would see the truth. Because energy doesn't lie. I thought that if I saw how some energy reacted with other energy, then I would be witnessing the truth. I wouldn't be confused by stories and explanations. I would have direct experience.

While this is true, what is also true is that the objects themselves don't lie either.

Objects are both particle and wave energy. We are both particle and wave energy. Both are true at the same time. It is our observation of the object that determines the reality of that object. Humanity collectively determines the nature of our world. We also determine the nature of ourselves. Gregg Braden describes this phenomenon as Belief Code 26 in *The Spontaneous Healing of Belief.*

> *"In 1998, scientists confirmed that photons are influenced just by being 'watched' and that the more intense the watching, the greater the watcher's influence on how the particles behave."*
>
> —GREGG BRADEN

Reality tries to grab you by your ankles.

MEANINGFUL DREAM

I woke up early. I had asked the night before to have a meaningful dream. Upon waking I said, "Well, where is the meaningful dream?" Then I went back to sleep. And I had a dream.

> *I was in Antigo, Wisconsin, and was trying to make my way back to my grandparents' house. I went through an area of miniature architecture models. I ran into two older ladies who were blue beings, mixing huge vats of white fluff. Three hookers helped to mix one vat.*
>
> *Then I moved on and continued to try to find the house. There was a lot of fog and I couldn't find my way. The ladies were going to a restaurant.*
>
> *Then there was water where the road should have been. I said to myself, This isn't real. If this isn't real, I could just walk on the water. So I did. I told the ladies they weren't real either. Then I screamed "It's not real!" and I woke up.*

There had also been a dream before that one.

> *A friend, Sherri, was sick and dying. She had cancer and was in a wheelchair with her helper. She put a cover*

over her head and was smoking. I told her to quit smoking. She said it didn't matter, because she was dying.

I was trying to buy groceries at a store but couldn't make my way past some men who were outside, and the mud in front of the store grabbed at my ankles.

Later when I looked at the dream, I thought, *Don't cover up. Take control. Change your life. Change what is real and walk on water. Get out of the mud. You have been lost, but you will find your way. The old ladies can help you, to a certain point.*

I was not being able to see because of the fog. There is a lesson in all things.

ROLES

Other people in our lives are only playing a role that we have asked them to play. John is in my life to teach me not to worry. I know that worry is a waste of energy and that it is not in the present moment. I will experience what I am experiencing until I don't.

Mother was in my life to teach me about vulnerability and surrender. I know that vulnerability exists inside of true power. When I learn the lessons from the experiences, others will no longer have to play those roles. When I truly love myself, I no longer have the need to experience the lessons about worry and vulnerability. Love releases the need.

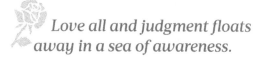 *Love all and judgment floats away in a sea of awareness.*

RIGHT AND WRONG

We need to embrace who we are, not dismantle it. Acceptance is the most powerful form of love. Acceptance is love. It is only the comparison with another that makes us right or wrong.

If I was alone on this planet, would there be anything to judge as right or wrong? Would I be too fat? Would I be wearing the wrong style of clothes? Would I be wrong about anything? Would judgment exist?

176

Judgment would not exist. Right and wrong would not exist. We are one, and yet we are alone, with our many selves. So why not live our greatest expression?

Receive, expand, and come back to a new self. Divine presence is in all things. We experience it through humanity. Seeing the luminescence in all things, we see the unique expressions of humanity that are the love and the light. They are not right or wrong. They are just expressions.

'I'm right. You're wrong. Here's my advice.' That's abuse. Where I fight against myself, that's abuse. It's still not okay. You can't move ahead from a place of resistance. You can't carry stuff around. You need to be with what you don't want to be with. The stuff isn't bad, just the resistance to it.

The belief around not having money. Notice when you need something. Or notice when you really want something. There is nothing that you need. You are already complete. You can't chase after happiness. Then you are running away from where you are. You are already happy.

'I don't want to be like this. Or I don't want that to happen.' When we resist it, it gets bigger, until we can be with it and don't resist it. When you remember that there is nothing to resist, there is nothing to resist anymore. You don't have to figure it out or understand it.

–ZACH REHDER

Judgments are self-induced illusions.

LIMITATION AND JUDGMENT

Judgments are not real—of yourself or of others. Judgments are a self-induced illusion. What are stories, emotions, and beliefs based on? They are based on the past or the future. When you bring the information into the present, it must change. Collapse the past and the future into the present moment.

Your body is 99 percent space. Of its 1 percent of matter, 70 percent is water. You entrained your genes for genetics. Your body's job is to make you right about yourself. What if you can only control limitation? You make a box and then you step into it. How do we get out of that box? Be the energy that defies the 3-D reality. Only that reality can be understood. And not even very well. Let go of understanding. Trying to understand keeps you in the box.

ENERGETIC TRASH

Our fixed positions activate us. We get affected by our own fixed positions. Our positions throw energy on us and it gets stuck there.

We live in the matrix of fixed positions. Move it back to flowing and allow the energy to expand. Use the knowing to harmonize the beliefs.

You have to go somewhere to find wrongness. Bring the disharmonized content into the present moment. Allow yourself to be with the bother, instead of asking, *Why is this bothering me?* Ask yourself, *What energy am I hungry for? Joy?* Thank the disharmonized content for what it has done and take out the energetic trash.

I hear Socrates saying, in Dan Millman's *Way of the Peaceful Warrior,* "Take out the trash, Dan. Take out the trash." Take out your energetic trash. Reside in the present moment.

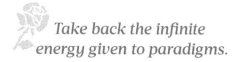 *Take back the infinite energy given to paradigms.*

WHISPERS FROM GOD

He wouldn't be bringing it up in me if I didn't need to release it. Why do I feel so wrong? Because it is wrong, not being one with God. Feeling separate, we feel wrong.

I hear whispers from God, or is it from my horse, or...? Sometimes it's a scream, and sometimes it's just a whisper. But at least it is authentic and comes not from a made-up mind but directly from the source: God, or any source in nature.

Can it come from the made-up things, divine objects created by humans? Aren't all things divine and divinely inspired? How or where can the divinity be found within the atrocities of the world? How can we know the purpose of life's experiences?

I would not change any of mine, even if I could. I can only change my life's experiences going forward. Let God write through my mind's meanderings so that I may know the Truth. Let his knowing flow through me so that I might share that knowing with the world, and with myself. Or at least let me know the Truth.

What do I know? I know that love abides in all things and that I must be truly present to experience that knowing and that love. It is a trick to stay present. All holding is a clinging to what has passed and pulls you out of the presence of knowing. All words and explanations are in the past.

> *Knowing is a stream of consciousness without punctuation.*

LISTEN TO AND RESPECT YOURSELF

I was listening to an interview with Don Miguel Ruiz. I had read all of his books and found him to be very real in his simplicity. He said that beliefs are just judgments and definitions—that beliefs are limitations.

We attach to lies. The momentum runs our life. We should be skeptical, but listen to everyone and ourselves. We disrespect ourselves when we believe everyone else's lies.

He said that we should observe and not react. Then we should decide yes or no.

MATTER AND SOLIDIFICATION

The whole conversation around what matters happens in the mind. Rikka talks about high-vibrating glasses of water and low-vibrating glasses of water. The lower-vibrating water raises to the higher vibration. But they don't combine and go to a medium vibration like matter does. They only go from lower to higher.

But if that were true, after billions of years, wouldn't all water be high-vibrating by now? Isn't it more a metaphor for unity and all things returning to God, which is the highest vibration of oneness with all possibilities? For God to know itself, pieces break off and separate for the joy of playing, experiencing, and knowing itself. Caught up in the experience and wishing to go further in the experience of knowing, choice and judgment set in. The more judgment sets in and matter solidifies, the more difficult it is to return to God.

Some even forget and believe that they are the center, and that they are what matters. We make things matter and then they solidify.

> *Every belief system is superiority to God. You think you know better.*

BELIEF SYSTEMS

What if everything happens because of your belief system? What if cause and effect are not real? What if it's a question of choice and no choice? Did the belief system actually create the experience?

You are an infinite being. You already are all the molecules you eat. So how can you be energetically affected by the food you eat? There is no cause and effect. There is only belief about what is cause and effect.

To undo the paradigm of being left behind, undo the feeling of being left behind. Tap into the feeling of oneness. Choose from the space of oneness. Ask questions. *Is this person someone I want to be friends with?* Do this from the space of oneness. When you are in the paradigm, you only have the energy of the box. Undefine yourself.

If you say, *I want this and I choose it,* you repel it with your wanting. It's like when a person wants praise and is needy about it. He says, "Did I do okay? Did I do okay?" The last thing you want to say in that moment is, "Yes, you did great." There is a lot of resistance to giving in to that kind of a need. No amount of your telling them will reassure them anyway. They need to tell themselves. The neediness creates the repelling feeling, even if you want to say the seemingly compassionate thing.

Expectations are also repelling. Let go of expectations.

You can't receive something from someone else. That would require separation. You are only shifting your own experience with yourself. Yes, with force is a contraction. Yes, with ease is expansion. The willingness to surrender is a doorway.

Be in the world. You are this ever-present being that can flow through everything, but not reference yourself from it.

The more you step back from the need, the more knowing steps in. You are not walking through a wall, you are walking through yourself. Knowing is a vibration within you. You are being your knowing. Matter is around beliefs. Play from the space of being. Be fun, joyful, playful, and adventurous. Be infinitely caring. Be total space. No one controls you from that place.

> *Knock down don't-know,*
> *so that you can function in the*
> *world of knowing.*

PASSINGS

We give events value. We try to make them matter when they are only "passings." They truly have no matter. What if only love matters?

How do I know? I do not know how I know, but I do know. Knowing is both solicited and unsolicited. We just have to listen with all our senses. We listen with our ears, our eyes, our hearts, and our flesh. Sometimes we get pain. We notice pain and it gets bigger, until we sit with it and ask it why: *Why are you here?* Or until we can simply be present with it. All of which is calling us into the present moment, where no pain or illness can abide. Only the love and power of the universe abides there.

All judgment is a contraction and a shutting down of energy. It locks us into the past and keeps us out of the present. The universe is always expanding and we are expanding with it. If we try to stay in one place we cut ourselves off from the universe as it expands and we feel pain, loss, and abandonment. Everything in the universe is showing/telling us to return to expanding with the universe, and asking us to join in the fun and joy of playing in the infinite consciousness, in whatever way we choose to feel and know God. We choose our experience that we are having on earth. It is up to us to have a good time.

Live. Laugh. Love! In this moment. And in every moment. There is only this moment!

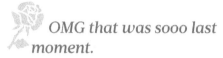 *OMG that was sooo last moment.*

TRIPPING INTO NOT MATTERING

This morning I was walking past my husband, who was sitting in front of the fireplace in his easy chair with his feet stretched out. I tripped over his foot. I saw myself fall on my back in slow motion, on the hard tile floor in front of the fireplace.

I didn't hurt myself. I am grateful for that. I saw each bump on my leg and knee as it occurred.

I lay there for a while. I had my hands full of supplies because I was setting myself up to write. I had a box of Kleenex, my glasses, my notebook, and a pen. I got up and just thought, *Hmm. That was interesting.* A few minutes later I was writing in my journal. I asked myself, *Why did that happen?* I almost never fall and certainly not in the house. Everything happens for a reason, right?

Then I told myself no. There was no reason and nothing matters anyway. Then I thought, *What if I tripped so that I would know that nothing matters?* The reason is to show me that there is no reason. Or, nothing matters. Now there's a paradox for you.

Exercises for Truth

1. Bring your heart into your mind or your mind into your heart. Both work. Do the one that seems easiest to you. Breathe. Reach up into the highest vibration that you can find. Breathe. Reach down into the center of the earth. Do this three times. Then find your center at your heart. And bring your mind down into your heart. Let your awareness expand out and function from this state. You will find that you speak the truth from this place.

2. Do the Morning Prayer. Ask God to show you what Truth looks like. See, listen, feel, and hear. Notice Truth throughout the day.

The **Snake** *winds and unwinds.*

CHAPTER 17

Notice Divine Perfection

MOTHER-IN-LAW TONGUE

I was picking up the laundry baskets to take downstairs. There were five laundry baskets stacked up on top of each other, and I was getting them out from behind a Mother-in-law Tongue plant. It's also called the bedroom plant, because it breathes at night and gives off oxygen when you are sleeping.

I noticed that the top basket was crushing one of the plant leaves. I thought, *Oh, no, John was careless again. Once again he didn't pay any attention to his surroundings.* So I told myself, *Maybe it was dark and he didn't see it, or he was in a hurry.* Both of which are almost always true.

I grumbled and started taking out the next basket, when I noticed that I had hooked the webbing of the basket on the plant. I stopped and realized I had almost injured the plant by pulling off its leaf. I had just been judging John for not paying attention, when the plant had grabbed hold of me and my judgments. What divine perfection the universe is, if only we care to notice it. My mother-in-law passed on several years ago, but her "tongue" is still wagging at me to not judge her son.

What do we mean by divine perfection? I sometimes feel, when something is happening, that it is neither divine nor perfect. But I now know that all things happen in divine perfection. We may not understand that they do or know the reasons why. But often God has a better plan for us and if we would just chill out, we might notice it while it is happening.

You can't plan what the universe has planned for you.

THE EASY LIFE

I've often felt guilty that I had such an easy, beautiful life filled with love. Others have had it hard. My little problems don't even hold a candle to the tremendous hardships of others.

Things haven't always gone my way, of course. I didn't always get the job that I wanted. I didn't always have money. Sometimes we were poor and didn't have much. But there are always people who are much richer and much poorer. Who has it easy and who has it hard is relative.

In 1971 I sold my blood in Europe to have enough money to travel. My passport and all my money was stolen out of the back of my backpack. I was on a bus going from the airport to a youth hostel in Rome. All I had was $5 hidden under the soap in my soap dish.

I left my backpack in a locked cage in the hostel and went to the American embassy to get a new passport. When I got there they told me that I needed someone who had known me for ten years to swear to who I was. I didn't know anyone so I went to a bar and picked up three sailors. After buying me a few drinks they were willing to swear that they'd known me their whole lives.

So back we went to the embassy. And I got a temporary passport. This was in 1971. Things were a lot simpler back then.

Back at the youth hostel, with a temporary passport with a big red stamp over my face, I went to pick up my backpack and everything had been taken except one change of clothes and my sketching pad. I needed my drawing materials because I was going to sketch architecture throughout Europe. I had written myself a University grant to sketch architecture for the summer. Everything else was gone from my pack, but I had the $5 I'd hidden under my soap.

So I sold blood every couple of days and traveled throughout Italy, Greece and Turkey . I camped out and slept in abandoned buildings. I never felt poor. It never crossed my mind to go home. I wasn't even depressed about it. I was just amazed that people would take what little I had.

What I now know is that there was a contract when I came into this world. I would live an easy life. Blessed beyond all measure. I always considered myself as strong and persistent. I rarely let myself be the victim.

When I allow myself to feel like a victim, things become more intense. My husband does not let me speak. I am a victim. My mother does not let me speak. I am a victim.

I am a victim. I have chosen to be a victim.

At the same time I have always known that I was loved. I love myself. My mother loved me, over the top. John says she loved me so much that even my poop smelled good to her.

My grandparents and aunt loved me. My father loved me, although he didn't love himself. My brother loved me. My husband loved and still loves me. And all my boyfriends loved me when I was growing up. I have always felt loved.

Still, little by little, I shut down when people did me harm. I was bewildered. I put it aside, continued on, and lost a part of myself each day. I became invisible, not seen or heard.

I want more. I have shown up and have been seen as a success in the limited world of reality. Now I wish to fly and live in the truly magical world of heaven on earth. I try to remember who I am with every breath I take. I breathe in the wonderment and breathe out the love of my expression to myself and the world. I know that it is divine perfection.

We need to speak empowered words about ourselves. You not being totally there or perfect is okay. It's the process. Go through it and then give it to the world. The old life is saying, Will you love me back into love? This is total surrender.

Your worst nightmares are your biggest gifts. What could happen that I don't believe is possible? Let go of the fear response. What would I choose? Choose around awareness and make your awareness shift to

your choice. Open to space and possibilities.
    As you increase your vulnerability, you allow oth-
ers to experience vulnerability.

—RIKKA ZIMMERMAN

What others think of me is
none of my business.

VULNERABILITY

I am reminded of a conversation that I had in 1985 in Kolonia Pohn-pei. I was working as Chief Architect for the Federated States of Micronesia. I was sitting in a bar talking to a planner, who had a type A personality. I'll call him Tom. We were talking about the Peace Corps; we had both served years earlier, and John was at that time a Program and Training Officer, on staff.

I talked about our training going into the Peace Corps in 1969. We had what were then called "T Groups," a kind of group therapy session run by a couple of therapists who would determine at the end of a ten-week training program whether we were socially and mentally healthy enough to serve two years in the Peace Corps. John and I were deselected, along with two other volunteers. Henry (not his real name) was deselected because they thought he wouldn't stay and would quit. I was deselected because I ran around "bra-less." The therapist told me that if I offended Americans by being "bra-less," I would offend the Marshallese.

It was the end of the sixties, and I was twenty. The local women were practically topless. Believe me, it was no offense. The other volunteers, a group of about 30 people, were outraged and staged a coup. They said they would all go home if we were deselected. So we stayed. In fact, Henry went on to stay for fifty years: he married a local woman and is still there with his grandchildren. We have gone back twice, and John became the director of the Peace Corps in Samoa. I told this story to my friend in the bar. He got very angry, and said, "I suppose I have to tell some secret of mine now, huh?" I was taken aback. I didn't understand his anger.

Now I realize that in the telling of the story I was being vulnerable.

When we are vulnerable, people have a couple different responses. One response is that they allow themselves to be vulnerable also. The other response, if their fear doesn't allow them to be vulnerable, is anger.

Women are very good at telling secrets. Sometimes that is a sharing of vulnerability, and sometimes it is just gossip. When you are vulnerable, you are open to all possibilities. This allows the universe to respond to you.

Creating this book is accepting vulnerability. Publishing the book moves from acceptance to celebrating it.

What does vulnerability have to do with divine perfection? When we are vulnerable, we are open and let go of resistance to negative outcomes. We are in the place of truth. From that place we can see and experience the divine perfection in all things.

THE BIRTHDAY GIFT

We celebrated my birthday last night. Actually, we celebrated both of our birthdays. John and I were born six days apart, the same year. We went out to dinner at a fancy restaurant, Che Fusion. We were seated in a tight little corner, because the restaurant was very full.

We were so happy to be there. The room was festive and full of people celebrating Christmas and the holidays. The table next to us was a huge table with a family who were celebrating with good cheer. It was a little noisy but we enjoyed our dinner and ordered champagne.

When the table next to us was leaving, John struck up a conversation with the woman. He told her how wonderfully her kids had behaved and what a nice family she had. She apologized for making so much noise and said that she hoped she hadn't ruined our evening. We said no and wished her a Merry Christmas.

Shortly after, the waiter brought us another bottle of champagne and told us that the woman at the next table had paid for our dinner. She left before we could thank her. What a pleasant surprise.

Happy birthday to me. Happy birthday to us. Happy birthday to Jesus and the world. Bad table or divine perfection?

I had recently been noticing divine perfection and cosmic coincidences. Sometimes events happened that seemed wrong or negative; I resisted them, judged what was happening as wrong. I thought it should have happened differently. I thought my plan was better. I didn't allow for the divine perfection that was actually occurring.

You can't plan what the universe plans for you.

DIVINE PERFECTION: WOOD PILE

One morning in 2015, I was looking out my kitchen window when I noticed that the door on the horse camper trailer was open and swinging in the wind. *Darn*, I thought. *I have to get bundled up and go outside to close the door.*

So I did. I went and closed the door. It was a beautiful day. I paused and took a deep breath. On my way back, I stumbled over some sticks of wood. They were just what I needed to start the fire in the fireplace that morning. Now I wouldn't have to go all the way out to the wood pile to fetch wood. The Universe was giving me just what I needed. If I had just grumbled my way back in and not taken that deep breath, I wouldn't have noticed the wood. I would have been in the past, still resisting, and not in the present. Being in the presence of the beautiful day allowed me to stop long enough to notice what was at my feet.

STEPPING INTO POWER

One day, I was experiencing some leg pain. I entered the pain and asked it what I should know about it. My answer: the leg pain was about stepping into power and letting go of control. And now, as I sit here typing this section, my leg is in pain. A couple hours ago I twisted my knee. Then I took the opportunity to sit down and write this section of the book.

MORE DIVINE PERFECTION

A while back, I spent a month listing what magic occurrences happened each day. At night before bed, or in the morning during prayer time, I would list ten happenings of the day that I considered to be

magical: cosmic coincidence or divine perfection, I didn't differentiate between the two.

At first it was difficult, because I was looking for the big cosmic
occurrences. Then it became easy, because divine perfection came
down to my being here with my breath. The breath is such a magical
occurrence.

Try making a list of ten incidents of divine perfection, every day
for one week. When you do this exercise, you will begin to look for
these incidents, and then you will notice them as they occur. What
you notice also changes: from the grandiose to the simple things.
Appreciating the simple things also seems to attract the more magnificent ones.

THE VOLCANO

On a Hawaiian trip early in the summer of 2015, I shared a condo
with a few friends. We had signed up for a retreat that was can-
celled due to the presenter being ill. We decided to go anyway and
have our own spiritual retreat, because we would have lost too
much money trying to cancel our reservations. We stayed in Kona
and decided to take a trip across the Big Island, to see the volcano
on the eastern side.

We started out fairly early in the morning. They asked me to be
the navigator. I said no initially, since I tend to get lost easily, but they
insisted. So off we went.

There are only two roads across the island. We had to take one or
the other. I took us on the coastal road. After we had traveled for a
while, our driver complained that we had taken the wrong road. It
wasn't the one he had intended. Since it would be a couple of hours
backtracking, we decided to keep going.

After another hour along the road, we came across an accident
on the highway. The accident was a bad one. It was obvious that
people had been killed. When that happens, the Hawaiians shut
down the road, to clear the debris and also to honor those killed in
the accident.

We thought about going back and taking the other road. But it
would have taken us about four hours, and by then it might be too

late to enjoy the volcano. We also had other things on our list that we wanted to see, including a double waterfall. We turned around. On the way back we came across a road into a small town, which we took. We decided to have lunch, and after lunch we were wandering around town when we came across a rock store. We had been told about this amazing store, because among other things it had the largest chunk of crystal quartz in the world.

So we stopped in. Leslie bought me a pink quartz crystal heart as a gift. The others were pleased, because we never would have found this store on our own and it had been on their list of things to do. I am not much of a shopper, but I like to look. We sat on comfortable couches and listened to the owner tell us about life and her gems.

When we left the store, we ran into a policeman. He told us that the highway was cleared and that we were okay to travel on in the same direction that we had wanted to go. Hmm, divine perfection. We weren't inconvenienced in the least. And we found something wonderful as a result.

We drove on and enjoyed the beautiful waterfalls. A little while later, we were driving around the eastern side of the island and about to head up to the volcano when my friend saw a magnificent monkey pod tree, standing in a cemetery. She had been searching for that tree for several days; she had seen it on a previous trip and she wanted to share the experience with us. But she couldn't remember where it was. And there it was. So we enjoyed the monkey pod tree, and wondered what amazing, miraculous thing would happen next.

On we went, up to the volcano. We hiked the steaming hot spots for a few hours until we got to the caldera, just as the sun was setting. Most people go to the caldera at dark, when it is most spectacular—so again, our timing was perfect. God's timing was perfect. We enjoyed Pele's light show, and then drove home on the other highway, wondering what amazing, miraculous thing would happen next.

We passed close to the bottom of the observatory, where we pulled over to see the billions of stars that can be seen at the top of the mountain—none of which would we have seen if we had taken that route in the morning, of course. The moon, which wasn't quite full, was below where we were standing on the mountain. It felt so strange to be above the moon. We admired the magnificent display and drove home wondering what wondrous thing the universe had in store for us next.

We had actually said the phrase out loud: "I wonder what magical wondrous thing will happen next." We said it after each occurrence. And it did. Now I say it every morning before I get up.

THE DANCE OF DIVINE PERFECTION

It was during breath work with Zach Rehder—in Kona in October 2015—that I truly felt divine perfection. This experience occurred after three days of breath work. At the end of each session, he asked us to share a phrase that described our experience. My phrase was "divine perfection."

Floating in the primordial soup and being very much in the present, I came to see that all events are perfect in their timing, level of intensity, and content. Life is dancing with us. We take a step and life leads. Do we follow? Is it a tango or is it a waltz? God asks me, "Will you dance the dance of divine perfection?" I say, "Yes." "And will you dance it here? And how about here, and even over here?" "Yes. Yes. Yes," I answer. "I will dance the dance of divine perfection with you."

Sometimes we have an experience and it is not what we would have chosen to do or be. If we are aware that everything happens in divine perfection, we might realize that things have turned out better than we could ever have hoped. God has a better plan for us than we do. If we know that, we are less frustrated when things seemingly don't go our way. It is divine perfection. And it is a dance. Enjoy the dance.

We can't do more or create faster than God.

Exercises for Noticing Divine Perfection

1. Make a list of past incidents that you thought were bad but then turned out to be for the best.

2. List the incidents of divine perfection that occurred that day. Try to notice ten. Do this for one week.

3. Do the Morning Prayer. Ask God to show you what Divine Perfection looks like.

4. When you get up in the morning, say, "I wonder what wondrous, magical thing will happen today." Then notice it. Repeat, as often as you remember, throughout the day, *I wonder what wondrous, magical thing will happen next?* Then watch it happen. Give gratitude when it does.

The **Giraffe** *reached down with his long neck to eat.*

CHAPTER 18

Co-Creation Matters

I recently sat down to work on this manuscript and my computer had crashed. I rebooted it and dashed off to the bathroom. When I came back, I noticed that I didn't have my wristwatch on. I always wear it. But I sat down to start writing again, when an ad for wristwatches popped up on the computer. Was the computer reading my mind? Was I was reading the computer's mind? Perhaps it was just co-creation.

What is creation? How do we create or manifest? Are things ordained? Is it fate? What choice do we have as human beings? People around us seem determined to create a negative experience. We have the choice to buy into their negativity or to create the experience we want to live. We choose, and the universe offers us more choices, and we choose again.

> *The more you live in the past, the longer it takes to make a change.*

3D OR 5D?

The time is 2012. The third dimension, or 3D reality, is where most of us operate from. The fourth dimension is time, where we create instantly. The fifth dimension is the state of unity consciousness, where you exist in the love of God and co-create with the universe. It is synchronistic and magical.

Let go of the double bind of time. How is it a double bind? Because we try to live in both the past and the future. Live in the present and ask for support.

VISION: A FOOT IN BOTH WORLDS

I see a woman with a cape. The cape has a hood and I can't see her very well. I am the woman with the cape. She glides down the stairs of an obviously old castle. The stairs are cold and made of stone. At the bottom she turns to the right. There is an opening onto a field. She is Snow White. She carries a blue bird. Then the woman twirls fast. She zooms into the air and flies around.

I have my eyes open. One foot is in this world and one foot is in the other. I have to maintain both in order to see.

A crow shows up and flies near. I realize my path is to have one foot in both worlds. This is true power and sorcery.

UNCONSCIOUS COMPETENCE

We manifest from unconscious competence. This is very similar to a conversation I had during a horsemanship clinic with Robert Goodland. He said that the goal is to act from a state of unconscious competence with our horses. We do this so that we know what to do, when to do it, and why. It takes practice and knowledge to act from unconscious competence.

FOUR STEPS TO UNCONSCIOUS COMPETENCE

1. *Unconscious incompetence.* You don't know what you don't know. Oblivious.
2. *Conscious incompetence.* You know what you don't know. Seeking.
3. *Conscious competence.* You know what you know. Aware.
4. *Unconscious competence.* You don't know, but you know. Consciousness.

When considering unconscious competence from a spiritual point of view, there is a balance between why and how. *Why* exists in the state of being. *How* exists in taking action.

We often get stuck on both the *why* and the *how*. Our story about why doesn't matter. Our asking how doesn't matter. What matters is the state of being, unconscious competence. We manifest from unconscious competence. We practice, model, witness, pretend, and then have an "aha" moment. The "aha" is a higher self-embodiment. Then we create. When we create from this place, it is co-creation.

ANGELS ANONYMOUS

Notice what happens when you are open to receiving. Support is in the universe, not in us. We don't have to do it all by ourselves. Allow people who can contribute to show up in your life.

Fear is never stopping me again. I learned not to expect so much, so that I wouldn't be disappointed. I learned to do everything myself. Do I have do everything myself because nobody else is good enough? I will do anything not to have the human experience. I belong to Angels Anonymous. "Hello, my name is Tricia, and I am an angel." Let's go to that meeting! And here's my 18 step program. Each chapter is an aspect of God and is one of 18 steps. Co-creation is one aspect of God and one of the steps that we can take to come home to ourselves.

The brain entrains with the heart. The heart has a bigger electromagnetic vibration.

MANIFESTING

We manifest by aligning our energy with the universe. Then the universe aligns with us. Then we align even more. And the universe aligns even more.

I'm thinking about manifesting a Porsche. What do I do? I don't think about not having it. I think about having it.

It's just like getting into the vortex. I look forward to creating with the universe. I find something to feel good about and then get out of the way. I don't want to interfere with the universe.

Care more about love than in being right. Let go. "I'm going to use the fact that you said that to me to feel bad. And I'm going to take that to my grave.

—ESTER HICKS

JUSTIFIED IN FEELING BAD

Holly

I have two friends who cling to feeling bad. Holly (not her real name) estranged herself from her son over a comment he made about her house.

She has not spoken to him in ten years. She will not be the first to say "I'm sorry." She will carry that vehemence in her heart to her grave.

She may forgive him if he apologizes first. I have seen her do that. But she holds onto the feeling that she has been wronged. And by God, she is right about being wronged.

Debra

Another friend, Debra (not her real name), is estranged from her sister. Her sister wrongs her with every comment she makes, so Debra decided to not to speak to her.

Six months later, she tried again, but her sister was still hateful in her responses to Debra. Debra becomes reactive and hateful. She justifies her actions. Debra decides that she was right and her sister was wrong. The sister doesn't care what Debra thinks—she will go to her grave saying she's right, and so will Debra.

Debra continues to cling to being right, but she is willing to forgive her sister over time. The sister is not willing to forgive Debra, though. The sister is miserable. Debra is miserable. They could both be happy if they would let go of trying to be right.

HAPPINESS AS A CHOICE

Happiness is a choice. We can cling to "right" or we can be happy. We can choose unconditional happiness.

That doesn't mean that we don't feel other things. We do. We simply feel sad or angry until we don't, and then move on to feeling happy. If we can't let go of the story around our feeling angry, then we won't let go of feeling angry. The story holds the feeling in place. It will continue until we make ourselves sick. And then we might choose to let it go—or not, and then we go to our grave angry, sick, and miserable.

Or we could let the story and misery go and be happy. Going into the feeling and really feeling it allows it to move through us more quickly. Feel it until you don't.

Caring more about love than about pursuing conditions reminds me of an experience that I had while having lunch with Holly. We were at a Japanese restaurant. We were seated and had ordered our lunch. If anything could go wrong for Holly, it would. She thought the restaurant was too hot and thought we should leave. I said okay. I never argued with her. But we stayed.

The lunch came and of course something was wrong with it. She complained. She complained about the service and gave them a lecture about customers and service, which she always did because she believed that she was an expert. Sometimes they listened and sometimes they didn't.

When we went to pay our bill, there was something wrong with the bill. She didn't want to sign her credit card. The restaurant insisted that she did. She said she would never return there again. But we did. Up until a few years ago, she complained 90 percent of the time. Now it's probably 50-50. I had lunch with her this week. It was 30-70. There was a time when I would have been embarrassed by her behavior. Now I find it funny. I laugh and say okay. I love her anyway. I see the wonderful heart she has inside of her. My allowance of the behavior seems to tenderize its hardness. If I resisted it, she would only lock in her right to behave that way and justify it by the correctness of her position. I care more about love than I do about being right.

 *Source is expressed from within.*

GENERAL VERSUS SPECIFIC

Ester Hicks talks about being general when you are in an argument or headed in that direction. She suggests going specific, on the other hand, when you are in alignment and want to manifest something.

> *In an argument, go general. Move in the direction of never-ending joy of figuring out who you are becoming. The feeling of the vortex is calling you to the specifics of the manifestation.*
>
> —ESTER HICKS

NOTICING AND CHOOSING

The universe gives us a buffet of people, places, and things. We have free will to choose what we wish to notice. Thus—with our noticing, or some would say choosing—we co-create the universe that is in front of us.

But then how do we create something that we have never seen or known about? Something that we can't notice because it doesn't seem to be there to notice? We simply ask the universe, "What else is there that I might play with or know?" And the universe answers, "How about this?" A new animal, plant, place, person, idea appears in the buffet for us to notice.

Notice...question...notice...question. This is the catalyst for co-creation. Throw a little gratitude into the mix and we have magic.

Noticing starts the flow of energy. Gratitude increases the flow. Magic occurs when focused energy (noticing) is at a high level (gratitude) with intention (direction of will or knowing). Thus we, with God, co-create the magic that is our life experience on this earth.

ABOVE AND BELOW

What if instead of the moon moving the tides, the ocean, and the ocean that is inside of us, what if the oceans, when they rise and fall, really move the moon into its trajectory? What if what is really happening is backward from our understanding of it? And what if the oceans inside of us, which are our true feelings, are really "slingshotting" the moon and stars into their orbital trajectories?

I always knew we were affected by the moon and stars. What I didn't know was how powerful we are. I didn't realize how our feelings affect the moon and the stars. We created and continue to create the moon and stars moving around us! As above, so it is below. That has been our understanding. But what if it's really "As below, so it is above?" We create from the inside out, not the outside in.

CELEBRATE JUDGMENT

When we are seen, we are vulnerable to the world. By being vulnerable, we change everyone. Sometimes we are so afraid, we can't think or breathe.

Jump in anyway. By the end, you will be changed. What if all that energy is not fear, but energy that will change the world? Fear is only what is outside your comfort zone, what you are not used to. Change occurs not because of what you say, but because of what you are. Why would you create a blanket of judgment and then wrap yourself in it? So you can be right about your fixed perspective? My job is to show up and to celebrate my showing up. It is never to judge myself. Fire your inner and outer critic. How do you fire the outer critic? Celebrate when someone judges you. It is just an opportunity to let something go and to let go of pretenses. How do you fire your inner critic? Let go of the walls of your belief system. What future would you choose beyond your belief?

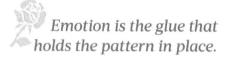 *Emotion is the glue that holds the pattern in place.*

BEING SEEN

I have struggled with being seen my whole life. I have played in two extremes: on stage, and in the back of the room.

I watch all that is going on in the front from the back. I love to see everything that is going on. I always give myself a reason for my behavior. I sit in the back, because I want to see everything. I can't stand to miss something. Could it also be because I don't want to be seen? I don't want to acknowledge that I am a player on the stage.

I did a little theater in college, small parts in plays, and drama chorus. I also taught college for twenty years. I got up in front of classes every day and lectured. I have given many speeches over the years. Most people thought I was extemporaneous. In fact, I was prepared. I planned and prepared all my speeches. Teaching stressed me out until I was well prepared and knew what I would say—then I could say what I needed to say and also speak from what I now know is my heart, from my knowing. I think well on my feet and was impassioned in my acting. I was considered to be successful.

At some point in my spiritual journey I confused letting go of limitation with being seen and heard. I wrongly thought that if I erased my personal history, got rid of any record of my existence, I would be free to change. I thought that it was my personal history that was locking me into my current present.

I got rid of records of my past. I refused to have my picture taken. When I retired, I asked that the college not put a brick with my name on it in the garden. It was the first time that anybody had ever made that request.

I wanted to pass through the earth without touching it. Or at least touching it as lightly as possible. I thought that those actions would free me from limitation. I thought that it was a waste of energy to hold a definition of myself in place. I thought that erasing personal history meant erasing limitation.

I chose to struggle with being seen. And now I don't.

Sometimes I think that I will publish this book under a pseudonym. That is my fear of being fully seen and heard. I think that I will change the names of family members, so that they will not be angry with me for being seen through the judgment of my eyes. It is not my intention to hurt them. Their journeys are their own.

I believe that because I am a private person. My journey is my own. I now let people take pictures of me. Sometimes I even enjoy it, especially if I can pose as something silly. I love silly. I also don't try to hide or create any personal records.

I began journaling. Before, when I had journaled, I destroyed them. I was afraid someone would read them. I am now using them to write my book. This is a part of my not erasing my past history. It is a part of being seen.

Demand that you and your being show up in everything that you do.

SEDONA: THE STAGE

In June of 2016, I went to Sedona to perform a thirty-minute session of my healing modality onstage. At that time, I had no idea what my healing modality was.

But I knew that I could tell a story, and that the story was something the other person needed to hear at that time in their life. It just worked that way. I also knew that I could take people on journeys and that they would find something that they needed to hear or see on those journeys. I could also play with energy and turn it into a kind of dance with my hands.

So that is what I did.

The Sedona Performing Arts Center stage was a major turning point for me in allowing myself to be seen. It was meant to be just that. It gave all of us Life Transformed Coaches a chance to stand up on a large stage and be who we truly were in front of an audience.

I would say that there is nothing more terrifying. But that isn't true. A hundred-foot wave towering over you or a lion chasing you would be more terrifying.

And actually, the stage, with people who are there to experience the love you are about to share, is not terrifying at all. It is exhilarating. You are full of more energy than you can possibly imagine, but you can still speak. And there is a calmness in the center of that energy.

BEING FILMED

Many of us crossed our edges that day and pushed some boundaries. I crossed several. One was being filmed.

I didn't want to be professionally filmed. That was part of my resistance to being fully seen. Not only seen, I thought, but to be held in posterity so that all could see it in the future, at any time.

I decided I wouldn't be filmed. After all, I was never going to use it, nor would I even show it to anybody, and I probably wouldn't look at it myself.

But them I changed my mind, a couple of days before the event. I asked to be filmed. I felt that if I didn't, I wouldn't be fully participating. And why was I there if I wasn't going to participate?

I also was convinced that I wouldn't watch it. I thought that I would just throw it in a drawer and never let anybody see it. Actually, I watched it right when I got it. I thought it was great! I still have some judgments about how I look, but I thought that I moved well. It was entertaining, and the content was great. I had fun. The audience had fun.

I love my life and I love me!

But I haven't let anybody see it yet.

SINGING AND TONING

Another boundary that I crossed onstage was toning. Toning is a melody or sound. Usually it doesn't have words but it has the energy to heal. I had limited experience, at that time, around toning. A melody had come to me in Bimini and then even more so in California.

I began singing it. Now I sing it all the time. I sing it almost every morning when I meditate and when I go to call the mares in from the field. The first morning I sang the song to the mares, Rhumba ran right up to me. My trainer was there, watching. She was amazed. I decided then that it would be the song that I used to call the horses in. And so it was. My trainer later asked me what recording the song was on and what the name of it was. I said it wasn't recorded; it was just a gift from God.

I started to tell my limiting story of how I couldn't sing when I was onstage. I wanted the audience to know how hard it was for me. Then I realized, after my toning, that it wasn't hard at all—that it was easy. And that any story that I thought was true about my singing was no longer true—and it had never been.

My made-up story was that I couldn't sing. My mother couldn't sing. In fact, she croaked like a frog. In church, people asked her to not sing, just to mouth the words. In grade school, at my first Christmas show, my teacher asked me to not sing and to just mouth the words.

After that, over the years, people said, "You are off key." "You changed keys." "You are tone-deaf." I would sing in the shower and to my plants in the garden and to my horses and to my mother, who thought I was great.

I married into a family of singers, who cared about perfect pitch. John, his mom, and both of his brothers are singers. So I was surrounded by musical wonders. In my younger years, I'd kept my mouth shut so as not to be criticized.

I took voice lessons in college. I played the piano. I wrote songs for each of my animals. I would sing the songs to them. I could *hear* the songs; I just couldn't make what I heard come out of my mouth.

Until I did. And then I knew I could sing.

So that is my story about why I couldn't sing. All of it happened, but none of it was true. Repeating that story over the years only built in the limitation and locked it in place. When I toned onstage, I realized that the story was no longer true. In fact, it was never really true. It was just that I gave significance to events.

And toning onstage was actually easy. I can sing. In fact, I was just singing a song the other day, when I noticed that it sounded really good. I thought, *Who was that singing, and where did that come from?* It came from me!

SHAPESHIFTING

Another boundary that I crossed onstage was shapeshifting. There wasn't any fear around this at the time; I hadn't even thought about it. There's more fear around it now, when I think that I had the audacity to shapeshift onstage in front of a group of people. And it is on film. But I didn't think about it then. I just did it.

I told them I would shift into a horse. That one was easy for me because I had been doing that since I was a child. I enlisted Pegasus, my spirit animal. And we did it. Some people saw some parts. Some saw others. Some saw the whole animal. Some will see it ten years from now.

I tried to hold on to horse for as long as I could. Many animals were thrown at me. All the spirit animals of all the people in that room and many others were thrown at me. I felt them all run through me at a rapid rate, all the while holding *horse*. So, was I a horse on the stage? Yes, and I was also a rhinoceros and badger and.... To me this is true vulnerability.

NAKED LIKE ME

I am reminded of the story of the emperor who had no clothes. He thought he did. But the people saw him as naked, and perhaps deranged.

My fear about this is that I am naked and perhaps deranged. Although someone wise once said that you must lose your mind in order to find it. I know that is true.

John had a dream not too long ago. In that dream...

> *He saw me standing up on a pulpit in a church. I was naked. But I was standing there perfectly calm, as if nothing out of the ordinary was happening. He was also naked, but he was hiding under a sheet that he had wrapped around him.*
>
> *He was sitting in the first row. I asked the people in the church to get up and stand in front of me. They were each dressed in their costumes, a policeman in uniform, a nurse in her uniform, a librarian, a businessman. They all wore cloaks of various positions and definitions in life. I asked them if they wanted to be naked like me.*
>
> *They did not. They were afraid. I was literally not afraid to be seen or heard.*

SPEAKING MY TRUTH

Speaking my truth has been a challenge for me. Speaking anything at all has been a challenge. Now I see that it is all divine perfection. If I hadn't gone through the story of not being able to sing, would I even care enough about it to try to sing? Am I pushed by having to prove something to myself?

Speaking and writing used to be things I avoided. There is a limiting story here too. My husband and mother were and are great speakers and writers. Mother was a beautiful writer and editor. She spent the first half of her career writing and editing and the second half working in mental health, to get stories to write about. She had a way with words.

My husband is also a gifted writer. So much so that I became too intimidated to even try to write. They both talked constantly. I had a hard time trying to get a word in, in either of their presence. Eventually, I quit trying.

I found that when I was away from them, I could speak quite well. Sometimes I talk too much: I am so excited, I just can't get it out fast enough.

Now, I am somewhat at peace with my husband's conversational style and don't let him take over my stories, or finish my thoughts or ideas, too much. I try to demand equal time. Mostly I speak when I am away from him.

One friend that I used to go to lunch with was also a talker. I wondered why I had surrounded myself with people who would not let me speak. I learned to listen. And that is a gift. I learned not to dissipate my energy by jabbering. And that is useful. I am grateful for those lessons.

But I often felt frustrated.

Now I am writing a book. Imagine that. *Hello, Mom. Hello, John. I am writing.* It is an outlet for my being heard.

I know that Mom is pleased. I started writing while she was alive. She was so proud of me. And now I am writing the book that she never did. The divine perfection in this is that I am motivated to push through not being heard, to speak and to write.

I look forward to creating
with a cooperative universe.

THE SACRED GARDEN OF SEDONA

Sedona has had further ramifications in my life. Often, when I do my Morning Prayer, I take myself to the Sedona stage. I reenter that space, physically, emotionally, and energetically. In horse training, we say, "Nose, neck, and maybe the feet." In spirituality, I would say emotion, energy, and maybe the physical. Some events that occurred originally come into my memory and then my being.

I address the group and the guides that were and are there now. Then becomes now and I try out my new ideas. *How about this,* I say, *or how about that?* Sedona has become a stage for me in the now.

Shamans have a name for the place from which you journey: "the sacred garden." Sandra Ingelman and Hank Wesselman refer to it as Grand Central Station. I like that image because from Grand Central Station you can take a trip to anywhere and anytime.

In the past I have had places in nature from which to journey: a lakeside, a river, and a meadow. I still use the meadow a lot. To get to the meadow, I go down stone steps and then turn right. I go out a cave opening and into a meadow. The meadow takes on various descriptions depending on what shows up, or maybe what I choose to focus on.

Buildings also play a large place in my dreaming. Maybe it is because I am an architect—or maybe I am an architect because buildings play such a role in my dreaming.

I love to dream spaces. I call that architectural design. The Sedona stage has become a sacred garden for me, a place from which to dream.

TIME

I think of the chicken and egg question as one of time. We can see the egg emerging out of its source and hatching into a chicken. Then the chicken reproduces itself. It makes sense. We can also see a chicken being brought into existence by Source and then reproducing itself by way of an egg—although two chickens have to be there for this to happen. Unless it's a divine conception.

It's odd to even entertain the question of virgin birth when you are talking about God in the first place. Time is an age-old question.

ARRIVAL

The movie *Arrival* portrays an alien species that visits the earth at twelve different locations across the planet. The aliens give different gifts to each of the countries. America is given the gift of time. The heroine is a linguist and she is partnered with a physicist.

Science, communication, love, and peace must win over war and fear.

Time is portrayed as a point, as linear, and as a circle all at the same time. In spirituality, we talk about the ever-expanding eternal now. That is the point. We appear to physically live in an expression of linear time. For space to exist, time must exist. You can't get from point A to point B without time and space existing. Most of us experience the space-time continuum as linear. The aliens saw time as more of a circle, with no beginning or no end. You can be on any point in the circle and can experience any point on the circle. It's continuous.

We usually see time as a continuous line. But in the alien's version of time, they could experience other parts of their experience at the same time; they could go forward or backward.

And so can we. That was their gift to us. Past and future don't really exist; they are only reference points for the experiences we are having.

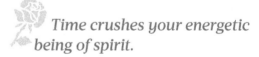 *Time crushes your energetic being of spirit.*

SPACE

Maybe we can understand time better in the context of space. A good example of the relationship between space and time is driving a car. How far do I need to be behind the car in front of me in order to stop, if they stop, before I collide with them? I need more space when

I am driving faster and less when I am driving more slowly.

I also recently saw the movie *Dr. Strange*. It's a comic book movie with nice visual effects of folding space: buildings folding upside down and inside out, everywhere in all directions all at once. It was like watching an Escher painting in 3D and animated.

The evil force was going to dissolve the universe as we know it, and the hero saved the day by folding space. He actually folded time also, to put the evil force in a continuous loop of time, as in the movie *Groundhog Day*, so that it could do no harm to the planet. This was a fun example of bending time and space.

As an architect, I design spaces. I love the concept of space. It is easy to understand the gap between points. The space between stars. The emptiness between our cells and the atoms and electrons whirling in space. There is also space between the notes in music, the quiet parts that give the sound more meaning.

THE FUTURE

We co-create from unconscious competence when we are willing to be seen and speak our truth. We choose unconditional happiness by letting go of story. We align with the support and cooperation of the universe. So why, in a book about turning heartache into Joy, in a chapter about co-creation, do I care about time and space?

Time and space affect our perceptions. They are intertwined. You can't have one without the other. They become the now, here.

What if you stepped into your future and saw that you were joyful? You didn't know how you got to joyful, but you definitely felt joyful. What if you then turned around to your past and saw that you were grief-stricken and full of heartache? What if you felt the heartache and joy at the same time? What if then there began to be no difference between the heartache and the joy? One is not better than the other. You love both.

What is here now? What do you choose to notice? There is only now and infinite possibilities.

I choose to notice Joy. Sometimes sadness shows up. Then I am happy to be sad. I love being able to feel all things. I love my sadness. Oops, it is no longer there. What is? Joy. Joy is nice too....

Exercises for Co-creation

1. Notice what is in front of you. Then ask the question, What else is there that I might play with or know? Wait and listen. Notice.

2. Do the Morning Prayer. Ask God to show you what Co-creation looks like. Notice throughout your day where Co-creation occurs.

Man *and* Woman
Co Create in harmony.

CHAPTER 19

Exercises for Transformation

CHAPTER 1: **Access Love:** *Go Through Fear*

Exercises

1. Place your anxiety or fear into a bubble and blow it away. Do this literally or figuratively.

2. Go where you don't want to go. Enter your fear or anxiety. Go there and feel it for 90 seconds until it dissipates.

3. Enter the edge of your comfort zone. Approach and retreat. Approach and retreat. Until you have a new edge.

CHAPTER 2: **Allow Love**

Exercises

1. Mirror work. Look into a mirror and tell your little one what s/he needs to hear. Ask her, "What do you need to hear about this?" Listen. And then tell her what she needs to hear. The answer will be something like: "I love you. I will keep you safe. You are beautiful." Look into your left eye in the mirror and tell her what she needs to hear.

2. Morning Prayer. Say whatever prayer you like and end with: "God, how much Love can I possibly be today? Show me how much Love I am. Show me how much you Love me." And then feel, listen, and watch.

CHAPTER 3: **The Way to Peace:** *Use Anger and Frustration*
Exercises

1. Say out loud three times. I commit to following my knowing.

2. Do seven seconds of breathing. Breathe in for seven seconds and out for seven seconds. Repeat three times. Reside in your heart as you do this.

3. Release your anger. Go outside and yell at a tree. Sit in your car and yell at your windshield.

CHAPTER 4: **Become Peace**
Exercise

1. Do the Morning Prayer. Ask God to show you what Peace feels like? Listen and feel.

CHAPTER 5: **Get to Joy:** *Feel the Sadness, Grief, and Loss*
Exercise 1:
5 Activities to Transmute Sadness into Happiness.

1. Ground every day

2. Body scanning. Where do your harbor sadness?

3. Emotional release. Feel your emotions until you don't.

4. Inner imaging. Let go of the negative stories and images.

5. Replacing the emotional exercise. Notice something happy or joyful. Place your attention there. But not until you have done the release. You don't want to paste happy onto sad.

Exercise 2: Rolling the Sadness into Joy

Think of something sad. Feel where the sadness is located in your body.

Is there a contraction or burning somewhere? Contract or lift the sadness up to your heart chakra. Let it drop back down.

Roll it up to your throat. How does it feel there? Let it go back down.

Roll it up to your third eye. How does it feel there? Let it fall back down.

Roll it up to your crown chakra. How does it feel there? Let it go back down.

You can also flow the energy in the other direction.

Notice your crown chakra and then notice your sacral chakra or wherever you are holding sadness. Then allow the energy from your crown chakra to flow down into the sacral chakra. How does that feel? Repeat for the heart, throat, and third eye chakras.

CHAPTER 6: **Express Joy**
Exercises

1. Do the Morning Prayer. Ask: How much Joy you can possibly be. What does it look and feel like? And then notice it throughout the rest of the day.

2. List all the ways that you have fun. How can you incorporate them into your home life, and workplace?

CHAPTER 7: **Reflect Beauty**
Exercises

1. Mirror work: Look into a mirror at your left eye. Tell yourself that you are beautiful. Find something that you can believe. If you like your hair. Tell yourself that you have beautiful hair. Do this for a few minutes. Do this every day.

2. Sit in a place of exquisite beauty or listen to music of exquisite beauty. Ask, why it is so beautiful? And listen to the answer. Know that it is only the reflection of your own exquisite beauty. Then check in about how you feel.

3. Do the Morning Prayer. Ask: "How much Beauty can I possibly be?" Ask God, "What does Beauty look and feel like?" And then notice Beauty throughout the rest of the day. When you see something that is beautiful, how does it make you feel?

CHAPTER 8: **Live in Harmony**
Exercises

1. Infinite perception. Repeat the following statement out loud three times:

   The more I have no idea of who I am, of what life feels like, of what I feel like, the more joy, magic, safety I am.

2. Pick a day and celebrate it for no reason. Do this once a month.

3. Flow energy down your spine as if you were a huge tube. Send it across each chakra, where you have placed a ball. Swirl the energy around those balls clockwise and counter-clockwise. Start the energy at your heart chakra and send the energy out and around in all directions. Work your way up and down your chakras.

4. Move energy in a triangle. Open your palms and see the sun above your head, and your mind and spirit in your palms. Circulate the energy around the triangle.

5. Move the energy in a figure eight, like the infinity symbol. Visualize the past to the left and the future to the right. The present is in the middle. Run the energy around it. See if you can spin the figure eight horizontally into a Taurus. See if you can spin the Taurus vertically so that it becomes a ball with a center point. All energy leads in and out at the same time. Play with it.

6. Morning Prayer. Ask God to show you what Harmony feels like. *Show me how much Harmony I can be.*

Then listen and feel. Notice when Harmony shows up throughout your day.

CHAPTER 9: **Act in Grace**
Exercises

1. Say, "I am love. I am light. I am infinite." Say, "You are love. You are light. You are infinite." Say each three times. Notice the difference. Where does each phrase reside in you? Bring the two locations together into one source point and say the phrases again. You can also use this as a walking meditation. I use it on each step I take or each stroke I swim.

2. Bring your heart into your mind or your mind into your heart. Both work. Do the one that seems easiest to you. Breathe. Reach up into the highest vibration that you can find. Breathe. Reach down into the center of the earth. Breathe. Do this three times. Then find your center at your heart, and bring your mind down into your heart. Let your awareness expand out from this state. You will find that you will move with and in Grace.

3. Create an alignment button. Notice what direction your spirit is going in. Then hit your alignment button.

4. Say the Morning Prayer and ask to be shown what Grace feels like. Ask God to show you the Grace that surrounds you in life. Notice where it appears in the rest of your day.

CHAPTER 10: **Build Communication**
Exercises

1. For grounding: Feel into the earth with the energy of your feet. Tickle the center of the earth. Take a deep breath. Do this three times.

2. For knowing: Go into your heart. Expand out as big as the universe. Ask your heart what it knows about this.

Ask all of your questions from this place. Communicate from this place of knowing.

3. To communicate with animals: Open your heart and listen. Ask permission, listen, and give thanks. If you can't quite hear, turn the dial on the radio of your heart until you have the right frequency. It takes practice.

4. For opening: Say the Morning Prayer and ask to be shown what Communication looks, feels, and sounds like. Ask God to show you the Communication that occurs in your life. Notice how it appears in the rest of your day.

CHAPTER 11: **Heal with Love**

Exercises

1. To release judgment: Make a list of physical judgments you have about your body. What question does that judgment raise? Answer the question to release the judgment.

2. To let go of limiting beliefs: Make a list of pains or physical ailments you have in your body. Then make two categories. One is your belief about the pain, and the other is a message that the pain gives you. Act on the message. Let go of the belief.

3. Say the Morning Prayer and ask to be shown what Healing looks, feels, and sounds like. Ask God to show you the Healing that occurs in your life. Notice where it appears in the rest of your day. Is it in your body? Your mind? Nature? In others?

CHAPTER 12: **Grow Abundance**

Exercises

1. List all of your limiting beliefs about abundance.

2. List 10 things that are good about money . Where do you already have this in your life?

3. Where are you not good enough or lacking in your life? Journal on this for 15 minutes. Meditate for ten minutes on the perfection of your being.

4. Say the Morning Prayer and ask God to be shown Abundance. Ask God to show you the Abundance that occurs in your life. Notice where it appears in the rest of your day.

CHAPTER 13: **Give Gratitude**
Exercises

1. Make a list of ten things you are grateful for today. What are you most grateful for? Do this for thirty days.

2. Do the Morning Prayer. Ask the universe to show you what Gratitude feels like. How much Gratitude can you feel? How much Gratitude does God have for you? Listen and feel.

3. Play the Get to Game with yourself. Say "I get to do this" instead of "I have to do this." See how that changes the way you feel about what you are doing.

CHAPTER 14: **Brew Magic**
Exercises

1. List ten things that happened today that you consider magical or cosmic coincidences. Do this for twenty-one days.

2. Do the Morning Prayer. Ask God to show you how much Magic you can be. How much Magic is in your life? How Much magic does he see in you? Notice the Magic that happens in your day.

CHAPTER 15: **Explode into Bliss**
Exercises

1. Do the Morning Prayer. Ask God to show you what

Bliss feels like. Ask God how much Bliss you can possibly be. Can you see it, feel it, taste it, or hear it? Make sure you start with a great deal of gratitude. The gratitude will turn into Joy, which turns into Bliss.

2. Let go of control. Let go of any definition you have of bliss. Allow whatever shows up. Embrace it. Show gratitude.

3. Relax your body. Ground it. Run hoops of color up from your feet, as if they were a fine mesh. Each one a color of their chakra and each one becoming more refined. Go from your feet up over your head. Add a couple extra hoops that are pearlescent in pink, gold, and silver. When you are relaxed, grounded, and the energy is moving, say *I am love, light, and infinite.* Then notice.

CHAPTER 16: Speak the Truth
Exercises

1. Bring your heart into your mind or your mind into your heart. Both work. Do the one that seems easiest to you. Breathe. Reach up into the highest vibration that you can find. Breathe. Reach down into the center of the earth. Do this three times. Then find your center at your heart. And bring your mind down into your heart. Let your awareness expand out and function from this state. You will find that you speak the truth from this space.

2. Do the Morning Prayer. Ask God to show you what Truth looks like. See, listen, feel and hear. Notice Truth throughout the day.

CHAPTER 17: Notice Divine Perfection
Exercises

1. Make a list of past incidents that you thought were bad but then turned out to be for the best.

2. List the incidents of divine perfection that occurred that day. Try to notice ten. Do this for one week.

3. Do the Morning Prayer. Ask God to show you what Divine Perfection looks like.

4. When you get up in the morning, say, "I wonder what wondrous, magical thing will happen today." Then notice it. Repeat, as often as you remember, throughout the day, *I wonder what wondrous, magical thing will happen next?* Then watch it happen. Give gratitude when it does.

CHAPTER 18: Co-Create

Exercises

1. Notice what is in front of you. Then ask the question. What else is there that I might play with or know? Wait and listen. Notice. Question. Notice and question.

2. Do the Morning Prayer. Ask God to show you what Co-creation looks like? Notice throughout your day where Co-creation occurs.

RESOURCES

Books

> *The Afterlife of Billy Finger,* Annie Kagan (Hampton Roads Publishing Inc., 2013).
>
> *Awakening to the Spirit World: The Shamanic Path of Direct Revelation,* Sandra Ingerman and Hank Wesselman (Sounds True Inc., 2010).
>
> *A Field Guide to Lucid Dreaming,* Dylan Tuccillo, Jared Zeizel, and Thomas Peisel (Workman Publishing, 2013).
>
> *The Four Agreements,* Don Miguel Ruiz (Amber-Allen Publishing, 1997).
>
> *The Golden Motorcycle Gang,* Jack Canfield and William Gladstone (Hay House Inc., 2011).
>
> *The Magic,* Rhonda Byrne (Atria Books, 2012).
>
> *Move Closer Stay Longer,* Dr. Stephany Burns (Navybridge Pty Ltd., 1993–2010).
>
> *Neither Wolf Nor Dog,* Kent Nerburn (New World Library, 2002).
>
> *The Spontaneous Healing of Belief,* Gregg Braden (Hay House, 2008).
>
> *The Law of Attraction,* Ester and Jerry Hicks (Hay House, 2003)
>
> *The Way of the Peaceful Warrior,* Dan Millman (New world Library, 1980).
>
> *The Third Jesus,* Deepak Chopra (Random House, Inc. 2008).

Videos and Courses

> Awakening Prosperity by Jack Canfield and Dawa Phillips

Websites

Abraham Hicks, Ester Hicks: abraham-hicks.com

Asia Voight: asiavoight.com

Christine Elder: ChristiEL.net

Clayton Nolte: structuredwaterunit.com

Jennifer Mclean: mcleanmasterworks.com

Kenji Kumara: kenjikumara.com

Leslie Black: heartawakening.ca

Nikole Kadel: nikolekadel.com

Panache Desai: panachedesai.com

Rikka Zimmerman: rikkazimmerman.com

Zach Rehder: zachrehder.com

GLOSSARY

Chakras: These are spinning vortexes of energy. There are usually considered to be seven: a red root chakra at the base of the spine; orange sacral chakra above the pubic bone and below the navel; yellow power chakra below the sternum; green heart chakra, located near the heart; light blue throat chakra over the throat; the navy blue third-eye chakra, located between the brows; and the purple crown chakra, on top of and just over the head. Some say that there are several more chakras that string above our crowns and down into the earth below our feet; most people are only concerned with the basic seven. It is thought that we store the energetic imprints of our life's experiences in these chakras.

Circular breathing: A form of breathing that is rapid and pulls on the in breath but just allows the breath to fall on the out breath. There is no pushing. There is no pause. The movement is circular.

Clairaudience: Clear hearing. To reach into another vibrational frequency and perceive sounds or noise.

Clairsentience: Clear knowing. To reach into another vibrational frequency and perceive information by feeling.

Clairvoyance: Clear vision. To reach into another vibrational frequency and see a vision.

God: The higher power as each of us comes to understand it. The source. Divine power.

Grounding: Incorporating our altered state of consciousness into our physical reality.

Holotropic Breathwork: A form of breath work created by Stanislav Grof that includes a rapid circular breath, music, and a form of artwork that induces an altered state of consciousness for healing.

Morphing: Shapeshifting into an animal or object, to experience the characteristics of that object and to learn its life's lessons.

Spirit guides: Energetic beings that appear as ancestors or angels to guide us on our path.

Toning: A melody, song, or sound that spirit has brought through us to create change and healing.

Transformation: Comprehensive change that moves one along a spiraling path, ever upward.

Yang: The masculine aspect of the universe. Having to do with action and sun energy.

Yin: The feminine aspect of the universe. Having to do with being and moon energy.

SPIRITUAL PRACTITIONERS

Ester Hicks: Ester is an inspirational speaker and co-author of nine books. She has presented numerous workshops on the law of attraction. She appeared in the 2006 film *The Secret.*

Nikole Kadel: Nikole is a facilitator of spiritual expansion. She leads mystical, dynamic excursions that allow people to connect with nature in such places as Bali and Tonga.

Kenji Kumara: Kenji is a spiritual leader, psychic, medium, energy healer of *Quantum Lightweaving.* He facilitates workshops to help people to heal, transform, and live the life of their dreams.

Zach Rehder: Zach is an international speaker, teacher, and healer. He supports others in their awakening process. He is a facilitator of breathwork.

Asia Voight: Asia is an internationally known intuitive counselor, animal communicator, teacher and author.

Rikka Zimmerman: Rikka is a global leader in consciousness. Creator of Adventure in Oneness LLC. She is also a singer and songwriter. She integrates unique toning techniques designed to shift the listener into a higher vibrational and energetic alignment.

ABOUT TRICIA JEANE CROYLE

Tricia is a licensed architect and Life Transformed Coach. Her life has centered on teaching, architecture, introspection, travel, story-telling, and horses.

Tricia received a BA from Macalester College in Minnesota, a BED in environmental design and architecture from the University of Minnesota, and an MOB in business from Silver Lake College in WI. She has spent a lifetime of inner awakening brought about by experiences in the Peace Corps, living and working in exotic places including Micronesia, Polynesia, Spain, and China, and traveling to sacred places such as Machu Picchu, Bimini, Sedona, Kona, and Nan Madol.

Through the years, she has made contributions to environmental protection, sustainable architecture, and education. She established Silver Creek Designs LLC as an architecture company specializing in sustainable and sacred architecture. She is an author, speaker, and life coach. She currently lives with her husband of fifty years, two cats, and six horses in Wisconsin.

CPSIA information can be obtained
at www.ICGtesting.com
Printed in the USA
LVHW030926201119
637820LV00003B/282/P